Approaches to Canadian History

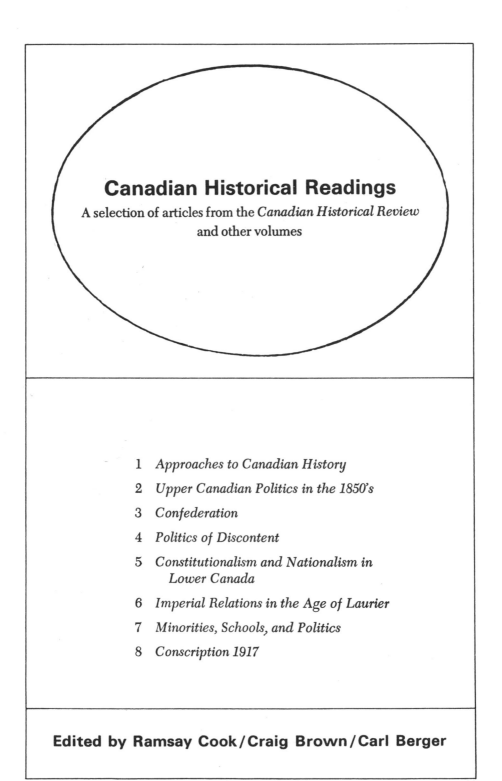

Canadian Historical Readings

A selection of articles from the *Canadian Historical Review*
and other volumes

Edited by Ramsay Cook / Craig Brown / Carl Berger

Approaches to Canadian History

Essays by W.A.Mackintosh /A.R.M.Lower
F.H.Underhill /W.L.Morton /D.G.Creighton
J.M.S.Careless /M.Brunet

Introduction by Carl Berger

University of Toronto Press

Printed in Canada by
University of Toronto Press, Toronto and Buffalo

ISBN 0-8020-1459-3
LC 23-16213

Contents

Introduction

CARL BERGER

THE HISTORY OF HISTORIOGRAPHY, properly conceived, fulfils a dual role. Its primary purpose is to make the reader and writer of history aware of the subtle and unconscious ways in which the very forces the historian seeks to interpret shape his own thought. "There are," as Herbert Butterfield put it, "hidden factors behind any national tradition of historical interpretation, and these need to be raised as far as possible to the level of consciousness, so that they can be neutralised or brought under control." In addition to sharpening the critical sense, the history of historiography may provide a penetrating insight into the intellectual character of an age. History has never been written with complete detachment; invariably it reflects and incorporates the ideological climate of the period in which it was conceived and composed. By studying the assumptions and guiding ideas which influenced the writing of history, one is really assessing the values and aspirations of the culture which produced it. Historiography, then, is both a means by which the element of relativism present in all history may be checked and a valuable tool of intellectual history.

Though Canadian historians have remained reticent concerning the philosophy of historical knowledge and have not engaged in such debates as that over relativism which shook the American historical profession in the 1930's, they have nonetheless devoted some effort to explaining the canons of their craft. A few of the following essays are tendentious in character; all are revisionist in intent. They critically appraise previous historical literature, and either propose ways of superseding outmoded points of view or advocate approaches which would add a new dimension to the understanding of the past. They are symptomatic of the shifts in orientation which historical studies have experienced and constitute a kind of capsule documentary history of Canadian historical thought. While the selection hardly reflects the total range of approaches to the past, these papers do suggest some of the major factors which have shaped the changing conceptions of Canada's history since 1920.

It is not the object of this introduction to recapitulate the analysis of the "schools" of Canadian history so succinctly outlined by J. M. S. Careless. There are three points, however, which should be borne in mind in considering these selections. The first is the question of why historical viewpoints change at all. To assign these alterations to some monolithic abstraction called the climate of opinion would be as simplistic as explaining them as automatic reflections of the material environment. Certainly such an explanation must include the fortuitous discovery of new materials, the impact of other disciplines such as economic history, the personality of the writer and his political interests, or the simple realization that hypotheses once dazzlingly brilliant in their novelty have become orthodox and fossilized. To appreciate how complex is the task of explaining changes in emphasis in historical writing, one need only ask, for example, why so massive an assault was launched upon environmentalism in the years following World War II, or why recent Canadian historiography has been so dominated by the biographical approach.

The second feature of these essays is the degree to which some of the central conceptions which have shaped the writing of history in Canada have been imported. Though the most obvious example of this borrowing is the Turner thesis concerning the role of the frontier in American development, the process is no less present in A. R. M. Lower's acceptance of the connection between the Protestant mind and the capitalist spirit first amplified by Max Weber and R. H. Tawney, or in F. H. Underhill's importation of the leading ideas of American progressive historiography as represented by Charles Beard and Vernon Parrington. The origins of metropolitanism run back at least to the work of Henri Pirenne on the rise of European cities, to a group of American urban sociologists who at the turn of the century did so much to establish some of the fundamental conceptions in the field, and to the books of the late Arthur Schlesinger, Sr., of Harvard University. Even the celebrated staple thesis of economic growth—perhaps the most original idea of Canadian social science—was dependent upon a way of seeing the economy which derived from the German historical school of the late nineteenth century. This derivative quality of Canadian historical thought is, of course, only one side of the story, but it provides an interesting parallel to the culture of which it is a part. It is impossible, in short, to understand Canadian historiography exclusively in national terms.

The third trait of historical writing in Canada is the way the various approaches to the past have become associated with particular views of the "national character." Patriotism everywhere imparted an enormous impetus to the study of history and an image of an heroic past became a major component of the sense of nationality. In less sophisticated days, amateur historians always justified their work—especially when they were appealing for government subsidies—by claiming that history instilled a sentiment of community and would bind the disunited sections of the Dominion together. Though generally more cautious, professional historians are still ultimately concerned with the character of Canada, with the distinctive elements of the nation's past. This concern arises not only from the unit of their study but also from the factor of commitment. As a result, the concepts employed to interpret the past have often become inextricably entangled with nationalism. The frontier thesis was accepted and then rejected not only because of its usefulness or irrelevance for explaining experience, but also because it implied a certain view of the national character. W. L. Morton criticized the Laurentian view not primarily because he felt it to be untrue, but because of its cultural implications for the residents of the hinterlands. A similar order of considerations also affected Underhill's reflections on the liberal tradition, Lower's expression of faith in French-English co-operation, and M. Brunet's rejection of the traditional interpretations of the Conquest. These papers, then, go far beyond the boundaries of what is usually thought of as technical history.

There is no comprehensive survey of Canadian historical scholarship. Apart from the items listed in the footnotes of the article by J. M. S. Careless, there are several additional pieces from which the story can be pieced together. J. K. McConica, "Kingsford and Whiggery in Canadian History," *Canadian Historical Review* XL (June, 1959), and C. C. Berger, "Race and Liberty: The Historical Ideas of Sir John George Bourinot," Canadian Historical Association, *Report* (1965), analyse the outlooks of two late-nineteenth-century figures. *The Literary History of Canada* (ed. Carl Klinck *et al.*, Toronto, 1965) contains two essays on history, one by K. Windsor covering the period to 1920 and the other by W. Kilbourn on recent developments. An interesting survey is presented in C. B. Macpherson, "The Social Sciences," in *The Culture of Contemporary Canada* (ed. Julian Park, Ithaca, 1957), and a bibliographical guide in Robin Winks, *Recent Trends and New Literature in Canadian History* (Washington, 1959). The character of economic thought and history is presented in Craufurd D. W. Goodwin, *Canadian Economic Thought: The Political Economy of a Developing Nation, 1814–1914* (Durham, 1961), W. T. Easterbrook, "Trends in Canadian Economic Thought," *South Atlantic Quarterly* LVIII (winter, 1959), D. G. Creighton, *Harold Adams Innis, Portrait of a Scholar* (Toronto, 1957), and J. B. Brebner, "Harold Adams Innis as Historian," Canadian Historical Association, *Annual Report* 1953. General surveys of French-Canadian historiography and social thought are Ramsay Cook's "French Canadian Interpretations of Canadian History," *Journal of Canadian Studies/Revue d'études canadiennes* II (May/mai 1967), and Jean-Charles Falardeau, *L'Essor des sciences sociales au Canada français* (Québec, 1964). Some of the individuals represented in this collection have extended their comments on the character of Canadian history. These may be found in D. G. Creighton's presidential address in the Canadian Historical Association's *Report* (1957), in "Towards the Discovery of Canada," *University of Toronto Quarterly* XXV (April, 1956), and in "The Decline and Fall of the Empire of the St. Lawrence," Canadian Historical Association, *Historical Papers 1969*, reprinted in his *Towards the Discovery of Canada: Selected Essays* (Toronto, 1972); in W. L. Morton's *The Canadian Identity* (Toronto, 1961); in F. H. Underhill's *The Image of Confederation* (Toronto, 1964); in M. Brunet's "The French Canadians' Search for a Fatherland" (*Nationalism in Canada*, ed. P. Russell, Toronto, 1966); in J. M. S. Careless's " 'Limited Identities' in Canada," *Canadian Historical Review* L (March, 1969); and in A. R. M. Lower's *My First Seventy-Five Years* (Toronto, 1967). A critical estimate of Brunet is submitted in Ramsay Cook, "The Historian and Nationalism," in his *Canada and the French-Canadian Question* (Toronto, 1966). The theme of survival in both French- and English-Canadian historical writing is traced out by Cook in *The Maple Leaf for Ever: Essays on Nationalism and Politics in Canada* (Toronto, 1971), chapters 8 and 9. For a stimulating critique of Canadian historical writing in terms of the neglect of social classes see S. R. Mealing, "The Concept of Social Class and the Interpretation of Canadian History," *Canadian Historical Review* XLIV (Sept. 1965).

Approaches to Canadian History

Economic Factors in Canadian History[1]

W. A. MACKINTOSH

THERE will be few dissenters from the position that there is need that more attention should be devoted to the geographic and economic factors in Canadian history, and that greater place should be given to the continental aspects of Canadian history. Up to the present the constitutional bias has been strong, and for the obvious reason that the most recent and in many ways the most significant chapter of British constitutional history has been written in Canada. The familiar school-book periodization of the history of British North America in terms of succeeding instruments of government is sufficient illustration of this bias of the British constitutionalist. The artless query of a high school pupil, "Was everybody a member of parliament then?" indicates the false picture which has been too frequently drawn. It is true that of late years more attention has been given to the economic and geographic factors, but in many cases the chapters on constitutional development have not been in the least influenced by the addenda on "social and economic progress", or by the introduction on "physical characteristics". Constitutional crises lose none of their great importance when viewed as the periodic results of changing conditions, and of the needs and political prepossessions of various elements of the population. History is emphatically not "past politics"; it is the life of yesterday in the present.

[1]The present article contains the substance of two lectures in Canadian economic history given at the School of Historical Research at Ottawa during the summer of 1922. The thesis is presented as one which the writer thinks susceptible of proof, but which cannot be taken as proved until further research has established it on a sound basis. Much elaboration and obvious illustration have been omitted in order that the argument might be presented within reasonable compass. As originally given, the lectures purported to show the relation of economic and geographic factors to general history, and to suggest the great need for detailed research in many phases of Canadian economic history.

The point of view of the article has been suggested by the writings of Professor F. J. Turner and the late Professor G. S. Callender.

W. A. M.

Reprinted from *Canadian Historical Review*, IV (1), March, 1923

The simplest features of American geography are of primary importance in understanding the developing life of the people of this continent. The initial fact to be noted is that for several reasons, structural and climatic, North America faces Europe. That is to say, by far the greater part of this continent is most easily accessible from the Atlantic coast. This has facilitated, though not accounted for, the success of European rather than Asiatic colonization. The evolution of energetic, industrious, forthfaring peoples under the peculiarly favourable climatic conditions of north-western Europe is the most important element in that success. If then we start with the fact of the European colonization of the Atlantic coast, the structure of American barriers, plains, and waterways takes on a special significance. That structure shaped the course of westward progress; it facilitated or hindered the connection of the frontier with the older settlements and with Europe; it selected to some extent its own settlers; and together with other factors it determined the trend of industrial production.

Structurally, North America, in broad terms, is made up of narrow coastal plains on the Atlantic and the Pacific, the old glaciated Laurentian plateau around Hudson Bay, and a great Central Plain from the Appalachians to the Rockies, with no significant uplift barrier from the Gulf of Mexico to the mouth of the Mackenzie. The presence of the Appalachian barrier to westward movements of population and commerce has given premier importance to the existing gaps in that barrier, of which two, the Mohawk and the St. Lawrence valleys, outrival all others. The partial gaps of Pennsylvania, the Cumberland, and the southwesterly valley of the Shenandoah have all played important parts in American history; but New York to-day is witness to the significance of the Mohawk valley, as is Chicago to that of the St. Lawrence. When the Dutch and French controlled both gateways to the interior, English colonies built solid communities in the coastal and piedmont regions. Meanwhile the French followed the westward path of the St. Lawrence to discover the basic fact of modern Chicago, viz., that the low watershed causes the St. Lawrence there to pivot on the Mississippi, and on that fact France built a grandiose policy not of settlement but of empire: a policy which failed because of the weakness of the initial settlements.

When the forerunners of British settlement began to enter the central valley and speculative ventures such as that of the Ohio

Company about 1745 were set on foot, France and Britain in-evitably clashed. They clashed on the upper tributaries of the Ohio where France was busily constructing a line of forts to block British progress into the interior. In later years the war took a European name, the Seven Years' War. Hostilities, however, began earlier in America; they had a distinct American objective, and that objective was not Canada—which was scarcely prefer-able to Guadeloupe—but the Mississippi valley.

From about 1763 on, the rapidly increasing population of the old colonies overflowed into the Mississippi valley. New England, spreading north and west, entered the valley of the St. Lawrence in the Green Mountain state; and because of its geographical relation to Canada, Vermont did not enter the Union until 1791, ignored the Non-intercourse Act, and was an unwilling and half-hearted partner in the War of 1812. New York and Pennsylvania were already expanding along the Mohawk and the upper Ohio valleys and the men of Virginia occupied the valleys of Tennessee and Kentucky. New problems brought new movements, and the "men of the Western waters" became a significant element in American legislatures.

Later, and with different setting, the same movement into the interior took place in Canada. The American Revolution, the causes of which were not unconnected with the occupation of the west, turned part of the westward movement to the Loyalist settlements of the St. Lawrence valley. At the same time, and later, British immigration augmented the increasing population of the western frontier of Canada. That old West of Canada differed from the settlements of Lower Canada not only in race and religion but in the pioneer problems which it had to face.

In those brilliant introductions to his *Readings in the Economic History of the United States*, the late Professor Callender set forth the basis of colonial economy. "Progress does not take place unless the colony possesses markets, where it can dispose of its staple products. The history of modern colonization does not show a single case where a settled country has enjoyed any con-siderable economic prosperity, or made notable social progress without a flourishing commerce with other communities." The prime requisite of colonial prosperity is the colonial staple. Other factors connected with the staple industry may turn it to advantage or disadvantage, but the staple in itself is the basis of prosperity. The colonies of North America were fortunate in being capable of producing staples which for the most part found ready markets in Europe. Virginia and the other southern colonies found in tobacco, indigo, naval stores, and other products excellent colonial staples, on which the prosperity of the South and southern culture were based. In the north, French furs found ready sale, but the conditions of the industry brought few advantages to the settlement. New England and the Middle Colonies were less favourably endowed. Their products were not dissimilar to those of Europe, and the markets were small and uncertain. Hence the importance to them of the development of the West Indian trade, of which the trade in "rum and niggers" was an important part but by no means the whole, and which brought prosperity to the Boston of commerce and shipping before manufacturing New England had arisen. Nothing is more typical of colonial development than the restless, unceasing search for staples which would permit the pioneer community to come into close contact with the commercial world and leave behind the disabilities of a pioneer existence. Contemporary records abound with the tales of the projects of the faddist and propagandist of new staples, and much money and energy was spent on experiments.

In the tidewater settlements of the British colonies the problem, though not without difficulty, was fairly solved because transport was cheap and Europe and the West Indies comparatively near. In Lower Canada, part of the population was lured by the prizes of the fur trade to the unsettled, vagabond life of the woods, which combined with missionary zeal to spread French names from Acadia to New Orleans and the Mackenzie. The other part, vainly endeavouring to produce an agricultural staple, took on more and more the permanent characteristics of a pioneer community which has failed to rise beyond the stage of primitive diversified agriculture, a self-sufficient, conservative peasantry.

As successive waves of population moved into the Upper St. Lawrence and Mississippi valleys the problem intensified.[1] The Appalachian barrier intervened between the frontier and tidewater, and transportation became a dominant factor in American trade. Not only, however, did the eastern barrier of Appalachia confront the pioneer of the central valley with a new problem, but the possible products of the western country were limited.

[1] Readers familiar with F. J. Turner's *Rise of the New West* will recognize the writer's indebtedness to it.

In spite of innumerable experiments they did not extend beyond grain and timber products, both durable enough but bulky, ill-adapted to the transportation of that day, and with little possibility of becoming profitable staples in any way comparable to southern tobacco or cotton until phenomenal changes had been made in means of transportation. Much might be written of the attempts to establish other staples such as hemp in Lower Canada, or to concentrate the bulk of native products to transportable proportions. The potash trade, partially successful, but handicapped by the smallness of the market, the domestic whiskey manufacturing of Kentucky, still surviving in the hill districts, and the industry which gave to Cincinnati its early nick-name of Porkopolis, were all attempts to reduce the bulky products of the Central Valley to transportable size and to establish the greatly-to-be-desired staple.

These obvious facts of the work-a-day colonial world were the conditions upon which colonial policy operated. We have already noted the geographical unity of the two great valleys of the continent and the influence which that unity has had on the history of Canada and of the United States. Up to 1763 the St. Lawrence and Mississippi were linked politically. Marquette and La Salle discovered the easy portages between the river basins and the great river beyond. The Seven Years' War was a war for the central valley which the French had explored, but which the British colonists were ready to occupy. After the conquest, when the Guadeloupe-Canada controversy had been finally decided, the valley was not broken but united with the coast settlements. From 1763 to the Revolutionary War, North America was a free trade area, and the exploitation of it one of the most pressing questions. Disputes between home authorities and the colonies as to the regulation of that exploitation, as shown in the attitude of Shelburne and his successors, in prohibiting settlement west of the Alleghanies in 1763, was one, although only one, of the causes of the American Revolution. With the concession of independence by Great Britain and the establishment of the Mississippi as the western boundary of the United States, the St. Lawrence and Mississippi were divided, and North America fell apart into the protected regions which remained until the Reciprocity Treaty of 1854 partially restored free trade.

This period from 1783 to 1854 (limits more significant than the usual 1791 to 1840) embraces the great age of westward expansion. Though the days of sea-faring New Englanders and Nova Scotians were not yet gone, America turned her back on the Atlantic and entered the era of internal expansion. In that expansion, two factors are of prime significance: first, the barriers to westward advance; and second, the barriers making difficult the continued communication with the older settlements. From the first of these the United States in this period was singularly free. Once through the Appalachian barrier the great plain of the Mississippi gave an open road to the Rockies. Formidable obstacles in the shape of dense forests there were indeed until the open prairie was reached, but no great barrier. To the westward, Canadian settlements in the St. Lawrence valley met the impassable barrier of the Laurentian highlands, bordering the Upper Lakes on the north so closely that for half a century progress into the easily settled prairie region beyond was effectually blocked. The immediate consequences of handing over to the United States the Upper Mississippi valley, to which access from the St. Lawrence was easy, were to be seen in the bitter struggles of the fur trade, the vain attempts of Canadian traders to retain the western forts at the time of Jay's Treaty, and the losing fight of the singularly able North West Company with their better personnel of French and Scottish traders against the exclusion policy of John Jàcob Astor to the south and the ruthless competition of the Hudson's Bay Company to the north. In 1816 the Exclusion bill was passed, and the company which depended for its existence on the connection of the St. Lawrence with the west, was "submerged" (as one of the partners said) in the Hudson's Bay Company in 1821.

In her communication with the old settlements Canada was more fortunate. The St. Lawrence valley was a line of communication only partially open to the United States. The good fortune was however, not unmixed. The St. Lawrence linked the frontier of the west, not with expanding, well-developed communities such as the Atlantic states, but with a community whose commerce depended entirely on the interior and which was surrounded by a stable, conservative population, to a large extent self-sustaining, with laws and customs non-commercial, and giving rise to little commerce. There was for the St. Lawrence valley no manufacturing New England and no cotton-growing South. Further, though the St. Lawrence, the Ottawa, the Trent, and other tributary valleys gave an open road to the voyageur, the fur-trader, or even the incoming settler, the way was by no means open for the return traffic of the timber and grain products of the western settlements.

For a period of half a century the scattered Canadian settlements entered into strenuous competition with the other routes from the interior to the seaboard. The Potomac Company, the Pennsylvania route, and the phenomenally successful Erie Canal were met by the stupendous efforts of the St. Lawrence canal system. The Erie had the great advantage of being complete before the British had grasped the problem, and when they were still occupied with the commercially useless Rideau. Most significant of all, the Erie was not a separate system, but a means of linking the upper St. Lawrence system with tidewater at New York. The existing stage communications had made the Albany route familiar to Upper Canadians, and the early opening of the Erie gave to New York a quantity of traffic which Montreal could not hope to equal for many years; and ocean freight rates to and from New York long reflected the better chances of getting both out-going and in-going cargoes.

In Canada of the first half of the nineteenth century we have a country in which population was moving westward to occupy the Upper St. Lawrence and Lower Lake regions at the same time as, at a much more rapid rate, the population of the United States was moving in great waves into the contiguous Mississippi valley. The people of both of these regions, though not of identical origin and with varied equipment for living, faced the same problem, confronted the same deficiency for colonial prosperity, the lack of a compact, saleable, transportable staple. In the case of the United States, however, the early building of the Erie Canal, the effective connection of the Mississippi with the cotton-growing South, and the much greater and more prosperous coast settlements gave a value to grain and timber products not found in Canada. The Canadian settlements in consequence lacked the prosperity which Durham and other observers noted in neighbouring parts of the United States. Not only, then, was Canadian development frustrated geographically at the north-west barrier of the Laurentian plateau, but economic and geographic facts constituted a frustration in the east.

These were the conditions with which commercial policy had to deal. In the United States the producers of bulky products in the upper central valley developed views of commercial policy different from those of the cotton planter of the South with a staple not only readily transported, but with a European market undergoing phenomenal expansion. The course of the tariff history of the United States illustrates the changing policies which these conditions occasioned. Those conditions made the home market argument a powerful one in the middle and western states, while the commercial elements of New England and the planters of the South favoured free trade. It was this growing divergence in economic characteristics which formed the basis for the struggle between North and South whether the specific occasion might be the tariff or the extension of slavery. The divergence was one of conditions rather than of people, though in succeeding generations conditions produced diverging types of people also. Yet families like that of Henry Clay passed from the Carolinas to Kentucky. The Carolinian by descent becomes "Harry of the West" in a western environment. The free-trader by inheritance becomes a protectionist when confronted with a western problem.

The commercial policy of Canada was part of the British Colonial System. It became so in 1763, and after 1783 the system was more carefully applied. The old system, based on a theory of sub-tropical colonial staples, still continued, as seen in the projects in Canada for the growing of hemp and the regulation of the cutting of ships' timber. In addition, however, a newer mercantilism, directed towards cheap food and materials, was finding a limited expression, and the need for building a stable settlement was also apparent. One aspect of British policy is to be found in the attempt to substitute Canada for New England and the Middle Colonies in the West Indian trade. Another is seen in the encouragement offered by preferential duties on Canadian timber and grain. Both of these policies just failed of success.

Partly because of ill-adjustment of bounties and duties to specific conditions in the West Indian trade, as shown by the numerous complaints from Quebec merchants, and partly because inertia made it difficult to substitute satisfactory trade connections with Canada for the familiar New England trade, the West Indian trade did not take strong root in Canada, though it was somewhat more successful in the Maritime Provinces. The West Indian market for Canada was uncertain and difficult of access. Canadian production responded only slightly to a varying stimulus. In turn, effect became cause, and Canadian grain and lumber, uncertain and variable in supply, was unable to support the irregular West Indian demands. The results were bitter complaints from both colonies. The prohibition of trade with the United

States endangered the supplies of the British West Indies and put them at a disadvantage with the other islands depending on United States trade. The advantages of steady supply, of nearness, and of familiarity with the trade were clearly with the New England and the Middle States. When trade relations between the United States and the West Indies were broken off, as between 1826 and 1832, Canadian trade boomed and the western settlements flourished. With, however, the acceptance by Jackson of Huskisson's proposals, and the resumption of trade, the wave of prosperity subsided, and Canada once more strove with the task of Sisyphus.

Less need be said in regard to the failure of the preferential policy toward grain and timber. Dr. Shortt's *Imperial Preferential Trade* and his articles in *Canada and Its Provinces* have made that failure abundantly clear. Before 1825, the complete prohibition of colonial grain (when the price was below 67 shillings) made trade spasmodic and ill-organized. The setting of a fixed duty on colonial grain, and later the adoption of the sliding scale, made matters better, but the direct trade in grain was not great. During the forties, the point of interest was not so much Canadian grain as it was American grain making use of the newly built St. Lawrence canals and obtaining the advantage of the Canadian preference. Montreal interests favoured the free export of American grain through Canada after paying the Canadian duty. Sir Robert Peel's much-quoted words about Canada being an "integral part of the Empire" were repeated by the Montreal dealers to support their policy; and while the Canada Corn Law did not admit American grain shipped by the St. Lawrence route free, yet flour ground from that grain was freely admitted. This Act, which legalized much that had been carried on extra-legally, gave a fillip to the St. Lawrence flour industry; and the repeal of all duties on wheat and flour some years later was a staggering blow to these interests, since the trade depended on this artificial stimulation. The economic and geographic union of the upper St. Lawrence waterway and the opening grain country of the American west was obvious, but, as Montrealers pointed out, the lower outward rates from New York more than counterbalanced the higher rates from the interior to New York.

The withdrawal of the preferences brought a similar and worse collapse in the timber trade, which had been considerably stimulated by the protection offered, although here too the trade was spasmodic and irregular. Further, the timber trade had some of the peculiarities of the fur trade in its opposition to home-making and its absentee ownership, and brought some of the same unfortunate results to the regions affected.

From one point of view the preference system was merely a continuation of imperial commercial policy. From the point of view of western Canada, however, it was an attempt to over-come the natural obstacles of the bulky products of the St. Lawrence valley and assure them a European market. More effective than the preference toward this end were the substan-tially complete St. Lawrence Canals. The St. Lawrence lacked some of the advantages of the Erie. The volume of traffic was small and the outward rates from Montreal relatively high. Any considerable stimulus might have brought success, but economic events and conditions combined in the depressing years of the late forties to snatch success away. In 1850 British commercial policy had just failed to attain its object.

As the population of the United States spread across the Mississippi valley to possess it, new problems and new political forces arose in American history. The upper valley faced the same problem of the bulky products which confronted Western Canada. Thanks to the larger population, the rise of manufac-turing in New England, the opening of the Erie Canal, the ex-pansion of the cotton staple in the South, and the access to the south by the Mississippi, the United States solved its problem, though not without difficulty. Out of those difficulties in that period arose typical western forces. The adoption of protection, the opposition to "the money power" and the United States banks, the leaning toward "soft" money, and the pressure for internal improvements came out of western conditions of life. Triumphant pioneering democracy rose to its height in the election of Andrew Jackson, important less for himself than for the forces in American life which he represented. Crudities and lack of culture in that period there were, enough to excite the mirth of Goldwin Smith, but strength and national unity were also there. Confronted with nullification in Carolina and the extension of slavery in Kansas, those who stated and enforced the national position, were men of the west and the Mississippi valley, Jackson and Lincoln.

One looks in vain in Canadian history in the first half of the nineteenth century for any such triumphant movement of western forces. In the opposition to the Bank of Upper Canada, the division between the West and commercial Montreal, the disputes over the Clergy Reserves, and the land policies of the Family Compact, similar situations brought similar reactions, but there was no effective movement.   An easy explanation for this difference is the divergence between Canadian and United States "political nature".   The Canadian, it is said, has never in politics gone to the extremes of his southern neighbour, nor has he expressed himself so much in popular movements.   There is truth in the statement, but the difference is not accounted for. The pioneers of the American and of the Canadian west came from the same sources—the British colonies.   It could scarcely be argued that the addition of Scottish elements represented by men such as Gourlay and Mackenzie added soberness to political life.   Nor yet did English or Irish immigration bring steadier policies.   There was no Jacksonian democracy and no Jackson in Canada because up to 1850 western development in Canada was doubly frustrated, at the east by the difficulties of the St. Lawrence route, and the European market for bulky staples, and at the west by the impassable barrier of the Laurentian highlands.   Important as were the constitutional issues of 1837, particularly in the minds of argumentative Scotsmen, there was also a basis of economic failure.   Not the least of the distinctions of Durham and Sydenham is that they saw this.   Constitutionally, Sydenham was wrong, for he knew little about government. Economically he was right, for he knew much about business. When failure became more apparent in 1849, the Annexation Manifesto was a gesture of despair on the part of the most articulate portion of a frustrated colony.

The middle of the century brought a new era in Canadian history.   The Lord Elgin who recognized the necessity of granting responsible government freely was no greater statesman than the Lord Elgin (pupil of the singularly able Hincks) who saw a partial relief from frustration in the Reciprocity Treaty of 1854.   What the result of that treaty would have been had outside events been different it is difficult to say.   Combined with the improvement of land and water transportation, and the substantial rise in grain prices resulting from the Crimean war, the larger local market, which the treaty gave, brought relief to the blocked colony.   For more than half a century Western Canada had striven to reach the goal of colonial existence, the production of a staple export commodity.   With this period the country passed from a stage of primitive diversified agriculture to the one-crop stage, the period (in the phrase of the late Mr. C. C. James)

"when wheat was king". Though not without its variations
that period lasted until the end of the Civil War and the repudia-
tion of the Reciprocity Treaty. The various phases of that period
of abounding prosperity, with its railway politics, bank expansion,
and incidental protection, are sufficiently well known. Economically, Canada was passing out of the colonial stage.

It would be dangerous to attempt to trace the direct political
effects of these conditions. Constitutional difficulties, the supposed menace of an American army, the position of Quebec, and
personalities were all solid and significant factors in the coming
of Confederation. It is not unfair to say, however, that the
dynamic factor which necessitated a constitutional readjustment
was the expansion of Canada West in the fifteen years previous.
Prosperity and expansion underlay "Representation by Population". The St. Lawrence valley, the Grand Trunk Railway,
the grain trade were uniting factors in Canada. The expanding
west demanded proportionate weight in a *national* government.
Differences of race and of geography necessitated *federal* government.

This period of expansion saw the substantial breaking of the
eastern frustration of Canadian development. True, dark days
in the seventies and later followed, but once lifted from the
frontier stage, the community was changed. The Ontario which
turned to cheese, fruit-growing, and small manufacture during
the years of trial was a different community from that which
had depended on the uncertain support of the British preference
fifty years before.

There remained at Confederation the problem of the West.
The Laurentian barrier, making impossible the commercial connection of the St. Lawrence with the north central valley, continued to be the solid dominating fact of Canadian development.
There could be no Canadian Chicago because there was no meet-
ing of waterway and prairie to the north of the lakes. Grand
Portage at the head of Lake Superior, with its well-nigh impassable
trail to Winnipeg, was the sorry northern counterpart of Chicago.

In the last half of the nineteenth century, as from the beginning, Canadians found the easiest field of westward expansion
in the Upper Mississippi valley. Fifty years before they had
hoped that the necessity of St. Lawrence navigation would bring
the population of the American west into a working union with
Canada. Great as was the effort of the St. Lawrence canals, it
failed to accomplish all that was expected. The Upper Mississippi

valley was preempted irrevocably by the United States. After the Civil War there could be no question of that. In the years that followed it seemed that the maxim of Henry Tudor would be justified, and that the greater would draw the less. After 1870, the cream of the immigrant and native population was drawn off to the easily settled prairie regions of the Upper Mississippi. The New West of the Canadians was the American North West. The Canadian frontier was the American frontier. In that period all the vitality which a moving frontier absorbs from a people, and gives back again, was lost to the communities of Canada. The export of men was draining the very life-blood of Ontario rural settlements. Canadian development was once more thwarted by geography.

It is this western frustration of Canadian development that furnishes the background for the construction of the Canadian Pacific Railway, and for the "transcontinentalism" of present-day Canadian transportation. As first put forward, the Canadian Pacific project was an audacious, even a fool-hardy attempt to bridge the gap between Ontario and British Columbia; and from that point of view the gloomy prophecies that the road would not pay for its axle-grease were "safe and sane" judgments. Though the construction of the railway was a part of a contract with British Columbia, the justification of the railway, and ultimately its salvation, was the north central plain of the prairies. That portion of the railway which links Winnipeg with Lake Superior was and is the most essential part of Canada's transportation system. It gave the St. Lawrence valley access to a country capable of rapid expansion. Other parts of the railway system were important and essential, but none has had the significance of that section which overcomes the Laurentian barrier between the Great Lakes and the prairies. With the building of the Canadian Pacific and its coming to effectiveness in the nineties, just when forces external to Canada were bringing grain prices to higher levels, the western barrier was substantially overcome, and a period of phenomenal expansion set in. Once more a Canadian region by reason of higher prices for grain and improved transportation facilities overcame its physical barriers and entered a one-crop stage of agriculture, the stage of the world staple and of prosperity.

That period of expansion from about 1900 to 1913 was not only a period of growing western settlement, but a time of solid progress in almost all parts of the Dominion. It is as significant

for the Eastern manufacturer and the Northern Ontario miner
as for the Western homesteader. Canada had room for expansion
within her borders. A staple was exported to world markets; and,
as southern cotton started the wheels of American industry and
commerce in the nineteenth century, western wheat has permitted the initial step of the Canadian advance in the twentieth.
It was only one commodity, and there were many; but it was the
basis of that period of prosperity. The world staple primed the
pump of Canadian industry.

To Canadians of the present generation political writings of
fifty years ago read strangely. Annexation, commercial union,
Zollverein, Canada First, Imperial Federation, these have no
place in contemporary politics. We are less sensitive on these
points. It is difficult to realize that Canadians ever believed in
them. The difference is not in Canadians. It is in the economic
background. When frustration of Canadian progress was overcome, and a period of expansion resulted, Canadian nationality
was assured, and policies which cast doubt upon that nationality
fell away. For the first time in Canadian history, powerful and
effective western forces made themselves felt. For the first time
western problems became capable of solution. The end is not
yet; for the West still struggles in time of world-depression with
a bulky staple and a long transportation haul. But improvements
in transportation have made problems not insoluble. A new
factor has arisen in the existence of a manufacturing East. Another
is developing in the opening of the Pacific trade; and still another,
of unknown significance, will come into play as the forest frontier
of the north is attacked in earnest.

Canada is a nation created in defiance of geography, and yet
the geographic and economic factors have had a large place in
shaping her history. It is not contended that these are the only
factors. Others have been often and adequately dealt with. But
unless one is to consider Canada merely as a collection of racial
types and not as a nation, the basic facts of economic and historical geography can never be ignored. In Canadian history as
it is written, there is much of the romance of the individual,
sometimes significant and sometimes not. It behooves present-
day historians to perceive the romance of a nation in the story
of a people facing the prosaic obstacles of a colonial existence,
developing national traits, and winning through to nationhood.

Two Ways of Life:
The Primary Antithesis of Canadian History

A. R. M. LOWER

THE school-boy, with unerring judgment, picks out as the dullest subject of his acquaintance, Canadian History. Given the way it is usually presented to him, the school-boy is right. But need he be? Does his judgment arise from the intrinsic nature of the material? I do not think so. On the contrary, the historian of Canada has at his command exciting and diversified resources, if he have but the skill to make them diversified and exciting.

Foremost among them, surely, are the glaring contrasts upon which this country rests, its sharp antagonisms, the diversity of the groups within it, its unbelievable geography, the ringing clashes everywhere upon all the great fundamentals. The human scene in Canada, both in time and space, is as full of bold colours as a typical Canadian landscape. The painter has used these effects: if the historian cannot, but puts everything into dull grey, it is his fault if people pass him by.

Of all our clashes, who will deny that the deep division between French and English is the greatest, the most arresting, the most difficult? Here is the most resounding note in our history, the juxtaposition of two civilizations, two philosophies, two contradictory views of the fundamental nature of man. For the historian, to neglect it is to leave the battle line. I propose therefore to devote this paper, with what skill I can command, to a short exploration of this primary antithesis of Canadian history. Since it is nothing less than two historic ways of life that I am going to look at, it is especially necessary to keep in mind the warning against "the dilettante who believes in the unity of the group mind and the possibility of reducing it to a single formula."[1] Whatever I have to say will, I hope, be taken by members of both races in the same spirit in which it is uttered, with a wish to understand but no desire to wound. While I shall be as objective as I can, I am well aware that to one of the divergent groups I myself belong.

* * *

A paper of this sort, attempting to look at a few of the fundamentals upon which this country is built, with a view to securing some of that release of tension so necessary to our national well-being, should logically begin with medieval Catholicism and St. Thomas Aquinas, for no one who wishes to understand Canada will get very far until he has studied the medieval structure which a section of this country preserves with singular integrity. Failing the possibility of so comprehensive an approach, the movement which stands at the threshold of our present era, the Reformation, may serve as a point of departure. To that revolt against ecclesiastical metropolitanism, the medieval church, which had been rapidly disintegrating in the liberal world of the Renaissance, owed the renewal of vitality that expressed itself in the Counter or Catholic Reformation. In France, the first of our mother countries, the historical process was delayed for three-quarters of a century by civil strife. This gave to the religious problem a solution not in terms of compromise, as in England,

---

[1] Max Weber, quoted in Tawney, *Religion and the Rise of Capitalism* (Pelican edition), 256, note 7.

Reprinted from Canadian Historical Association, *Report*, 1943

but in those of the new Catholicism.   The French Reformation, when in the first quarter of the seventeenth century it at last began to formulate itself, soon showed that it was not merely an imitation of that of Spain or Italy.   It was French and northern.   It was not particularly intellectual or artistic—no earnest religious movement can be—it had little either of the subtlety or the cruelty of the true Latins beyond the mountains.   It was enthusiastic, serious, moral, evangelical.   There was about it none of the fireside comfort of Anglicanism, little of the cold selfishness of Calvinism.   It was a warm, human faith, full of visions and harmless miracles, strict in the standards of conduct it enjoined on its adherents.   For those whose roots lie in nineteenth-century Protestantism, it diffused a religious atmosphere which, save for its ritualistic and sacramental basis, is not difficult to understand: it was a kind of nineteenth-century Methodism in a seventeenth-century Catholic setting.   It was above all things missionary, and the missionaries it was to give the New World, the Brébeufs and Lalemants, were to become in the manner of their deaths, strong pillars of France in America.   Their shadows have loomed the larger as they have receded and today the proud memory of the martyrs gives to French-speaking Canadians a centre of loyalties and a support which their English-speaking fellow countrymen have nothing to match.

It was in the man who was to be the first bishop of Quebec and in the nature of the church he established that the French Catholic Reformation was most deeply to affect Canada.   François de Laval was strong-willed, haughty, eager for power, a puritan in morals, ultramontane—as was perhaps natural in a man whose younger days were passed among the confusions of the Fronde, with its tarnishing of royal power—jealous of the privileges of the church as opposed to the state, jealous of his rights as bishop, jealous of his personal dignity in the presence of the Governor. Such traits have many times been repeated among his successors.

The ecclesiastical system whose foundations he laid was never to falter in proper loyalty to the King but within the orbit of that loyalty was to become as strong as the state itself.   Education was in its hands from the first—as was inevitable in a period where education was universally a department of religion.   The priesthood under him was formed into a disciplined body of men who were not allowed to become incumbents of "livings," but remained missionaries—fighting troops to be moved about from station to station at the discretion of their commander.   The system still holds.   The instrument Laval fashioned has proved its strength and its worth.

After Laval's time, Canadian-born became more and more common among the priesthood.   This had its advantages and disadvantages.   The Canadian priests were at one with their people: they were the natural shepherds of their flocks.   On the other hand, they were provincials, with little experience except in their own small world.   Their culture contrasted unfavourably with that of highly trained Jesuits and Sulpicians from France, but this lag in culture in the period following the original immigration is a familiar story in all new countries, a stage that must be worked through as a new society forms itself.   It was as nothing compared with the asset of the curé's closeness to his people.   When the evil days came, he had been fitted to become their natural leader, their salvation in tribulation. He retains his place to this day.   A moment's glance at history should be sufficient to take all meaning out of that charge so often levelled by bigoted people that the French Canadians are "priest ridden."[2]

Laval built on natural foundations, for Catholicism of this popular, even democratic, northern type reflected the genius of the French people who came to Canada, the peasantry of Normandy and its neighbourhood, just as its close relation, Anglicanism, has suited the neighbouring peasantry of southern England, and as paternalistic and sacramental religions suit any peasantry. The life of the peasant is a series of ritual occasions— planting and harvesting, being born, coming of age, begetting, dying. The land has always been there and it always will be. Man's occupancy is transient and the individual is only one in a long chain from forefathers to descendants. All are one family, inter-related if not in this generation, in the last or the next. All give unquestioned obedience to the great mother goddess, the earth-mother, who can easily be made to wear a Christian dress. The restless strivings, the desire for change, "improve- ment," "progress," "opportunity," which we today take as the normal condition of life, are absent. Man is subject to nature and to nature's moods: he learns to acquiesce in the drought and the flood, the good years and the bad. As his animals and plants grow and come to harvest, so he grows and comes to harvest. His religion is among the simplest and oldest of all creeds, Catholic almost by accident.

The business of the peasant—or *habitant,* as he became in Canadian parlance—was not to make progress but to "make land": to "make land" many hands were necessary. Nature responded, as she always does. Practically all pioneer peoples are prolific, the transplanted French were especially so. There was lack neither of food nor function for every new child. A socially minded people saw no evil in being surrounded with their own and in the swift, steady widening of the family connection. Quite the reverse. They found happiness in life, not in things. A new and finer house meant less to them than sons and daughters growing up in the neighbourhood. If some died, others came: they would all meet hereafter. If some were lame or halt or blind, that was God's will. It was life that He and nature commanded, not the saving of life. This other-worldliness, still so marked in the countryside of Quebec, and not at all divorced from practical wisdom, was re-inforced by the immemorial teaching of the church: man's real life begins hereafter. A genuine belief in immortality works profound effects on the manner in which a people lives. Catholicism and the countryside, simple French peasant traditions, as old as agriculture, and the French joy in human companionship, came together into a strong complex which to this day shows little sign of giving way.

Yet for decades the countryside of New France was a neglected plant, overshadowed by the adventurous foliage of fur trader and missionary. Old France had men for high tasks but not peasants for export. Nor did the home-loving peasantry of a non-emigrating race wish to leave their native soil. The English separate themselves from home and family with ease—and often with relief: they dislike the cramping atmosphere of small communities. The French cling to the ties of mutual support: they dislike going away from the near and the familiar. They accept and enjoy the life

[2]It is well known that after the conquest, the habitants were very glad to escape from the obligation of the tithe, but that indicates no general dislike of the clergy, simply a healthy independence, which has been demonstrated on more than one subsequent occasion, as, for example, in the elections of 1896.

of small communities.   It is not surprising that only a few of them came to the new province, less than ten thousand, it is said, but all of them firm in their Catholicism and carefully guarded from taint or touch of heresy! From these all persons of French-Canadian race are descended.   The combination of a faith kept free from all possibility of contamination, of a close environment, the banks of the St. Lawrence, and this extraordinary degree of inbreeding, produced a stock whose homogeneity surely can have few parallels.   For the rest of us, with our multitudinous descents, this close-knit world is almost impossible of entry.   All its members have clouds of common ancestors, all have had identical historical experiences and all hold the same creed.   Even today, amid the complexities of the modern world, the degree of differentiation seems relatively slight.   All French Canadians are, as it were, the same French Canadian.

The process of forming a new people began as soon as the first children were born.   By the Conquest, it was for practical purposes, complete.   The seventy thousand Canadians of 1760, in a century of wrestling with the wilderness, had created a new society: one resembling the old peasant societies of France but with its own orientation, especially with its own family clans and its own passionate love of the land it had made its own and the soil it had won from the wilderness and the natives; a society entirely cut off from the rest of the world, turned inward upon itself to a degree few people of English speech can grasp; a society unbelievably parochial but in every sense a strong blood brotherhood.   This was the little world that was to crash under the triumph of English arms.   The heart of the French nation had never been in empire and it saw the vision of Champlain fade without regret.   But what of the children of France, the Canadians, those who had taken such firm root in the soil that was to pass under the alien flag?   What of them, isolated now in the hostile, Protestant, English continent of the conqueror?

It is hard for people of English speech to enter imaginatively into the feelings of those who must pass under the yoke of conquest, for, except in the Southern States, there is scarcely a memory of it in all their tradition.[3] Conquest is a type of slavery and of that too we have no memory—except as masters.   Conquest, like slavery, probably must be experienced to be understood.   But one can intellectually perceive what it means.   The whole life structure of the conquered is laid open to their masters.   They become second-rate people.   Wherever they turn, something meets their eyes to symbolize their subjection: it need not be the foreign military in force, it need not be the sight of the foreign flag, it may be some small matter—a common utensil of unaccustomed size and shape, let us say, taking the place of one familiar.   And then there is the alien speech, perhaps not heard very often, but sometimes heard, and sometimes heard arrogantly, from the lips of persons who leave no doubt that the conquered are in their estimation inferior beings.   Even the kindness of the superior hurts.

Nor does conquest sit easiest on the humble.   The educated may make their peace, learn the foreign language, and find many areas in common, but the humble cannot cross the gulf—they feel pushed aside in their own homes.   Hence it is that nationalism will always live longest, even if not

---

[3]Yet as late as the nineteenth century an historian like Freeman could draw a line between the Saxon people, with whom he identified himself, and their conquerors, the Normans.   In his writings the Saxons were always "we," and the Normans "they." The memory of conquest dies hard!

blazing up into fierce flame, in the hearts of the people, who will seek to maintain their own ways by the passiveness of their behaviour, and little by little, as opportunity offers, will edge forward into any chance space left vacant by their masters.

Conquest in the forces it sets in motion may be tantamount to a revolution. The conquered are so bludgeoned by fate that they come to find new spiritual springs of life. Something like this did happen in French Canada. French Canadians are strong as a group today not least because they passed through the valley of the shadow a century and three-quarters ago.

No one can suggest that the English conquest was cruel, as conquests go, or the English government harsh. If the French in Canada had had a choice of conquerors they could not have selected more happily. But conquerors are conquerors: they may make themselves hated or they may make themselves tolerated. They cannot, unless they abandon their own way of life and quickly assimilate themselves, in which case they cease to be conquerors, make themselves loved. As long as the French are French and the English English, the memory of the Conquest and its effects, will remain. Not until the great day comes when each, abandoning their respective colonialisms, shall have lost themselves in a common Canadianism, will it be obliterated.

Within the old régime the French-Canadian type was formed: all its history since has been merely a superstructure on the foundation then laid. Anyone understanding the conquered people and gifted with a sufficiently prophetic eye could in 1760 have foretold the attitude of the French Canadians toward conscription in 1941, or for that matter in 2041. In external affairs, including war, it is, was and will be, simply that of most of the other small Latin and Catholic peoples of the hemisphere who have been cut off from their parent stock and find themselves in a world that has moved far away from the pole about which they swing, they whose metropolitan centre is not London, or Moscow, or New York, but Rome. If we can understand the reactions of Ecuador or Paraguay to this northern world of Anglo-Saxons, Slavs, and Germans in which we live, we shall understand that of Quebec readily enough.

In the 180 years since the Conquest, new phases of the basic situation have naturally presented themselves. As numbers and wealth increased and as English parliamentary institutions were introduced, a new class grew up—the intellectuals who spilled over from the too abundant material for the priesthood into the secular professions, especially the law. In French Canada, where everyone likes to talk and to hear good talk, the lawyer, *l'avocat,* has had a field day. His opponent invariably being another lawyer, every election has turned itself into an oratorical contest and since a superbly convenient whipping boy has always stood ready to hand, it has been inevitable that every contest should involve him—*les sacrés Anglais,* the damned English. Is it therefore too much to suggest that every political fight from 1791 to the present day has had as its fundamental, if unexpressed issue, the English conquest? If the situation were reversed, the same would be true of us—as it is to some degree true in the Southern States. But why does the point need labouring? Does not the municipal government of the capital of our largest and wealthiest province turn on an even more ancient issue than the Plains of Abraham—on that obscure Irish skirmish, the Battle of the Boyne?

The French-Canadian intellectual, whether lawyer, journalist, or priest, has run true to type. He has lived in a world of ideas—or notions—but he has been better at talking, perhaps, than doing. He has had a difficult road, because for him there cannot be that free play of the intellect so naturally assumed by his opposite numbers in the English camp. His education has formed his mind before the world has opened to him and he has had to do his thinking within a system whose boundaries are rigid. The results have been the weak development of the objective studies, the slam-banging personal tone of French-Canadian journalism (which is also agreeable to the spirit of the French race), its sometimes rather tenuous connection with facts, but above all the shoving-over of discussion and emotion to another concept, that of the race. The intellectual, priest or layman, has been the protagonist of the race. It is a natural, if somewhat unhealthy role. Any virile group cut off from free expansion will necessarily turn inward and console itself with its own virtues. It will at all costs seek survival and an opportunity to break its bonds. This is the motive power behind Nazi-ism, Fascism, and "Japanese-ism": Germans, Italians, Japanese, all suffer from a species of claustrophobia. So do many French Canadians, marooned in an English continent. Like causes produce like results. The utterances of extreme racialists everywhere, whether in Germany or in Canada, come back to about the same thing. But it has been our good luck, here in Canada so far, that the extremists of neither race have captured control of the state.

Nevertheless as the outside world has pressed more and more on the French island in America,[4] racialism has become more and more self-conscious and has absorbed into its concepts more and more of life, so that today it is impossible to tell whether the race is the bulwark for the faith or the faith for the race. Possibly the latter. It would appear to the outsider as if the French church today could to some extent stand apart from its own spiritual significance as a manifestation of Christianity and find its function in binding together people of common blood and speech.

We English Canadians have not until recently been very much plagued by intellectuals. Most of them who have not been drained off into practical tasks, we have managed to ship to the United States. The French have not had that easy solution. Their society was completed long ago and there has not been a great deal for the intellectual to do except watch the English men of business tear it to pieces. The French intellectuals cannot enter into that world, any more than can our own. They can merely stand at the threshold, their sensitive souls lashed with the thought that they may be regarded by the bustling representatives of the conquering race as second-class citizens. Hence their discontent. Hence much of the explanation for the Papineaus, the Bourassas, the Chaloults, with the rather pathetic cry, repeated from generation to generation, for more "posts," more safe government jobs, free from the rude blasts of English initiative.[5]

But French Canada, even if its people so desired, has not remained frozen in Maria Chapedelaine-ish postures. Things do move. The most

---

[4]And how heavily it does press! Note how American persuasiveness has at last drawn the "Quints" out of their backwoods French environment and put them on a public platform singing English songs! The reference is to their appearance at Superior, Wisconsin, during May, 1943, to sponsor certain ship launchings.

[5]It is in the 92 Resolutions of 1834 and in one of Mr. Chaloult's speeches of May, 1943.

conspicuous change is the coming of industrialism and the swing from rural to urban.[6] In 1871, 80 per cent of the French people of Quebec were rural, today only 42 per cent are. One of the most interesting questions that confronts the social scientist is what urbanism and industrialism will do to the Canadians of French speech. Will this unique peasant structure, this strong fortress of the Catholic Reformation be able to adapt itself to the new kind of life? French Canada today is in the grips of the first revolution its people have ever known, the Conquest excepted, the industrial revolution. What will be the outcome of the clash of medievalism and modernism, of the régime of the natural law and the acquisitive ethic? Will Catholicism adapt itself? Can the countryside continue to send out its sons and daughters in such a strong tide that peasant values, the faith and the church, will continue to dominate the cities? Will the race as binding concept more and more displace the faith under the dissolving forces of urbanism? Will urban values work back into the countryside and give to rural Quebec, as they have already given to rural Ontario, a kind of suburban atmosphere? Will the forces of continentalism triumph over this strong fortress of localism? Will the international unions displace the Catholic? Whatever the future holds, the appointed guardians of race and faith will put up a good struggle.[7] The rural clergy will not be tempted overly much by the English shibboleth of a "high standard of living": they see the trap that lurks in that. They will not be too much in favour of high wages and only mildly of progressive and social measures, for their people have not yet reached the stage where they feel it necessary to be parsimonious of life. Heaven may not be quite as close as it once was and temporal values may be getting more emphasis than they used to do, but the group is still more than the individual, life still more than the means of livelihood, and the simple standards of the countryside will for a long time carry themselves into the cities.

II

From this exploration of French Canadianism one figure is absent, the man of business. With very good reason. Except in minor roles, he is an inconspicuous figure. If one takes his *Manual of Canadian Securities* and looks at the serried ranks of Directors listed therein he will find only a corporal's guard of French names. The explanation is simple. Here is a society founded under a philosophy that admitted only a subordinate place to the man of business and his pursuits, that, even in his luxuriant fur-trading days, managed to keep him more or less in his place and that by

---

[6]RURAL AND URBAN FRENCH POPULATION OF QUEBEC, 1871-1941

Year	Rural	Urban	Total	Per cent rural
1871	745,125	184,692	929,817	80.3
1881	806,960	266,860	1,073,820	
1891	No returns	....	....	......
1901	848,229	473,866	1,322,115	
1911	904,357	702,138	1,606,495	
1921	920,553	968,716	1,889,269	
1931	945,035	1,325,024	2,270,059	41.2
1941	1,107,380	1,587,652	2,695,032	41.7

Table from 1931 census, 1,755, table 35, and 1941, bulletin A-4. The total rural increase in Canada 1931-41 was 310,000 of which the French in Quebec contributed 162,000.

[7]In the last decade the French added to their population almost 70 per cent more people than those of British origin did to theirs, 553,000 as compared with 331,000.

historical accident was rather thoroughly purged of him. It is possible to find Catholic societies in which a degree of capitalism has prevailed, though it is to be suspected that in them Catholicism has been subject to very severe strains. Sometimes, as in nineteenth-century France, it has been shouldered aside. But in such a preserve of the church as French Canada, it would be vain to expect any striking development of native capitalism—except the special form of capitalism represented by ecclesiastical corporative organization. Both historically and today the weight of French-Canadian society is against capitalism. The values it seeks to conserve are quite other. The business man does not walk among the French as a god. Honours are paid not to the captains of industry but to the political, and especially to the ecclesiastical figures. I can see no end to English-Canadian domination of the machinery of production in Quebec except the abandonment by the French of their attitude to life and their acceptance of ours—either that, which they will not deliberately make—or the invocation of the power of the state to take over English enterprise and thus a slipping back into a more or less efficient paternalistic socialism, in which the intellectuals at last have all the *postes* they want as public factory managers.

No; for this characteristic phenomenon of yesterday, the business man, we shall have to turn to the other side of the house, where he may be examined in riotous abundance. Our first contact with him is shortly after the Conquest when he comes rushing in on the heels of the military. He is in a hurry. He wants to get things done. He has ends to gain, an object in life. That object is one comprehended only remotely by the peasant. From the first the New World has released in men the passion of greed. Greed in itself as a human quality the peasant can understand well enough but not greed erected into a way of life and fortified not only with the majesty of the law but with the sanction of a religion. Yet no other group has so systematically set up acquisition as an object in itself and made it the centre of a cult as have the men of business of the English-speaking world.

In 1760, the new creed had not gone as far as it has since, and there continued to resist it the older elements in English life, feudalism in its eighteenth-century form of aristocracy and certain sections of the Church of England. It was in the fighting and governmental services that these elements found their strongest expression. It was therefore these that were to have the best relations with the conquered Catholics. The weight of the English thrust into the conquered territories was not, however, to consist in officials and the military, but in men representing the new way of life, which had already appropriated for itself a theology by which it could rationalize its conduct. This way of life became dominant in Canada and remains so.

The connection between Protestantism, especially Calvinism, and material achievement has been the subject of much investigation. Wherever Calvinism has prevailed, societies largely committed to the acquisitive way of life have arisen. The coincidence seems logical, for while the spirit of acquisition is as old as man, Calvinism subtly reinforces it. The burning question it presented to its adherents—and in altered terms still presents— was whether God had elected them unto salvation.[8] There was no infallible

---

[8]Today this question is put in much terser and secular form: "Can I make good?" C. A. Beard, *The Rise of American Civilization*, makes the point that since about mid-nineteenth century, the ethic of success has dominated the older ethics: not "Is it

means of finding out but God might give a sign. And what more visible sign could the individual receive than that he should be prospered? But the sign would not come if one merely sat and waited for it. So the faithful set about each to his own individual duty, doing, as he believed, God's work. As someone has said, there is no more awesome sight than a churchful of Scotch Presbyterians upon their knees praying God to give them strength to do His will unto their fellow men, and then arising to go forth and do it! Calvinism created strong men, strong in their convictions, strong in their demands for elbow room to carry out their allotted tasks. But not men who were much concerned with their fellows. That was God's business. While the Jesuits were threading the wilderness to bring Christianity to the Indians, the New England Puritans were burning them alive in their own villages.[9]

In countless ways the Calvinistic type of Protestantism accentuated the motives of accomplishment and success. Everywhere it found its most congenial soil in urban areas, among the middle classes. In industry, it became the support of self-made men, men who "did not need the government to help them in *their* business," and in politics, it came to stand for *laissez-faire* and the policeman state. Its spirit reigned supreme in Victorian England, the spirit of drive, of providence and thrift, of smug success. How far it all was from the scriptural injunction to take no thought for the morrow!

Nowhere was the acquisitive ethic more at home than in the New World. There the field was open and nature invited exploitation. Hence the strong link between it, the Scotch or New Englanders, the staple trade, and the characteristic expression of the staple trade, the metropolitan-hinterland relationship. Traditions that might have held it in check were weak. Nearly everything sooner or later was bent in the one direction—the contempt of the older ideals and the intolerance that the new and the moving invariably manifests for the old and the static. The goal of material success passed over easily into success in terms of accomplishment or of power and in these forms afforded the driving energy that has mainly made America.

No one would assert that there have been no other aspects of life represented among the English-speaking population of Canada. Among our farmers many of the traits of peasant societies survive, and the antithesis between the country way of life and the urban has been almost as sharp at times as that between French and English.[10] Certain areas of English settlement come close to the French countryside itself in their conformity to older social patterns.[11] In the region of religious or cultural tradition there is the Anglican emphasis on service to the state and on the ideal of the gentleman; or the Scottish ideal of the learned man, the philosopher. Very prominent is humanitarianism, that powerful body of emotions, sentiments, beliefs, and actions, which has penetrated every nook and cranny

---

just, is it right?" becomes the question, but "Can I succeed?" To fail in the presence of the group emerges as the unpardonable sin.

[9]A century later the *bourgeois* of the North West Company were zealously supporting the first Presbyterian Church in Montreal but that church showed a conspicuous absence of interest in the activities at the other end of the fur trade.

[10]It had a large share in the Upper Canadian Rebellion of 1837, the Clear Grit party, and of course in the more recent agrarian movements, especially Alberta "Social Credit."

[11]See Dr. Enid Charles's article on Prince Edward Island and its population characteristics in *Canadian Journal of Economics and Political Science*, May, 1942.

of our Canadian life. It would be interesting to analyse the complex way in which these all twine around each other. But space does not permit. English-speaking Canada has fallen under these various traditions in about the same way as the United States, though at a retarded rate, for here there have been influences restraining their free play. For example, our continuing connection with Great Britain has provided some shelter for a class structure and a quasi-official church, the Church of England. For the first seventy-five years after the Conquest, this older English tradition—the "squire and parson" concept of society—made a strong fight of it with commercialism—as in its modern form it is doing again today, under the special circumstances of the war, with its strengthening of the forces of history. But it too became more or less assimilated to the dominant tone, as witness the business relationships of the Family Compact men, and left the field pretty clear for the exploitive and acquisitive attitudes, which had an almost unchecked run until a decade or two ago. There must be few English Canadians of middle life who were not brought up on the conviction that their business in life was to succeed, "to make good," "to get on," "to get to the top," "to amount to something."

Methodism, whose social gospel also opposed a certain counterweight to acquisition, split under its pressure. The industry and thrift inculcated by the creed brought worldly success to many of its followers, who trailed off into the acquisitive camp, taking with them the phraseology of simpler days and the shell of the old attitudes of brotherhood and often leaving awkward gaps between profession and performance. But the genius of Methodism continued to assert itself in characteristic social movements, temperance, social service, and so on. Eventually it found logical expression in a more or less formal political socialism: much of the drive in Canadian socialism comes out of Canadian Methodism and as it does battle with Canadian individualism, it carries forward the Christian ethic of support for the weak and the lowly against the strong and the established.

These are the two most significant traditions at work in our English-speaking community today: they represent its sharpest antithesis, and the future will witness a battle over which shall organize it. Neither one is now very firmly attached to its original religious base. The Methodist-humanitarian tradition satisfies itself with a social gospel and a social task: it resorts easily to perfectionism—to Utopianism, pacifism, a vague internationalism, and a "planned society." The Calvinist-individualist-success conception of life, stripped of its fine phrases about election unto salvation, initiative, individualism, being nothing more than mere selfishness, was the first to run beyond Christian bounds. Those who live in this area find themselves today confronting life either on the basis of a rather mechanical benevolence and simple good fellowship or face to face with a frank hedonism and a stark paganism.[11a]

The dynamics of acquisition have transformed the world but the societies dominated by them—of which our own is one—despite their brilliance, are hollow at the centre. For deep in the heart of this way of life there seems to be a denial of life. It sets up for itself a goal of goods, of plenty, of a "high standard of living," and here finding common ground with humanitarianism, surrounds itself with devices designed to smooth out life's ills, to make life easier, to prolong and save life. It secures food and

---

[11a]The American divorce tradition, which is paganism, is a descendant of the individualism of American Puritanism.

shelter of an excellence never before attained. It increases the span of life, makes individuals healthier, stronger, taller, more alert. It decreases illness, physical disabilities, infant mortality, maternal mortality. And yet solicitous as it is for the individual's well-being, the societies it has created are slowly withering. Speaking of the disappearance of the English from the Eastern Townships, the authors of a recent book on Quebec say: "A peaceful victory, a grand victory, for today there are 300,000 French there as against less than 50,000 English. Note that the relations between them are excellent because our people have not returned the blows which their ancestors received. . . . 'The French are right to act in this way: it is better (instead of retaliation) to give the English splendid funerals' . . . . The majority of the English have become a population of old people . . . who having sold their property to the French, live in retirement in the villages. These villages present as it were 'the foretaste of a cemetery'."[12]

Many people become indignant because they would say the French are pushing the English out. I cannot see that the French are to blame. They are a virile people who can see no virtue in childlessness. If we have no instinct for group survival and choose the easy way out of comfort and race suicide, we have ourselves to blame.

Our two Canadian ways of life exemplify the antithesis that in general terms might be put somewhat as follows: The nearer what might be called the peasant-spiritual, or rural-natural, the primitive outlook on life, the stronger the hold on life, the greater the survival value of the group, the less considered the individual, the greater the complaisance in taking what life brings, good fortune or bad, good health or bad, sound limbs or crooked. In contrast, the more in the other current, acquisition, materialism, commercialism, urbanism, individualism, Calvinism—call it what you like—the greater the parsimony with life, the more concern for the individual, the more strenuous the efforts to keep him from blemish, to make perfect specimens, to patch up the defective, to prolong life, the less ability to create it. *The "high standard of living" seems to destroy life.* The one complex, in its extreme, leads to mere animalism, the other to extinction. Where is the happy medium and what philosophy will support it?

In Canada, the two outlooks have had marked geographical correlations. The urban-acquisitive complex has deepened in proportion to the longitude west. Prince Edward Island and Nova Scotia have been less affected by it than Ontario, Ontario than Manitoba, and Manitoba than British Columbia. Under the weight of the depression this tendency is not now so marked. The English in Manitoba and Saskatchewan alike are decreasing, and in Ontario and British Columbia they are being kept afloat by immigration from other provinces. In Saskatchewan the pattern stands out with especial clearness: in the last ten years, those races close to the soil have held their own despite misfortune—Ukrainians, Germans, Hungarians, etc. But the commercial races—those who do not see life as existence but as opportunity—have gone sharply down in numbers, the English, the Syrians, the Jews, and the Chinese.

There is also a decided religious correlation. Believe it or not, you will have a considerably larger family if you are a Pentecostal than if you are a Presbyterian. The further one moves away from the simple, rural,

[12]*Notre Milieu* (Montreal, 1942), 98.

pietistic groups, such as the Mennonites, among whom there were in 1931, 159 children under the age of five for every 1,000 persons, into the more sophisticated, urban, middle-class, acquisitive areas, which make large demands on life, the less is the likelihood that his group will replace itself in the next generation.   At the extreme stand the Christian Scientists, just where one would expect them, with 45 children under five per 1,000, the perfect embodiment of prosperous middle-class dessication.   When its characteristics are analysed every denomination falls exactly into the anticipated place.[18]

Correlations of group survival value may in fact be made by the bushel. There are positive correlations such as the rural life, pietistic or authoritarian religion, religious dogma, pioneer areas, old static areas, poverty, short life-expectancy, religious communism, communal segregation, lower class, labour in new industries, possibly aristocracy: and negative correlations such as urbanism, size of urban unit, individualism, altitude in the middle class, commercial attitudes, professional occupations, income, divorce, "feminism," the size and newness of automobile, exploitive economies, such as the mining and logging economy of British Columbia, suburbanized rural areas, humanitarianism, possibly agnosticism, intellectualism.   In general it is the humble who have survival value.   It is the meek who shall inherit the earth.

It is an ironic commentary upon history that that group which began with a return to life, with a triumphant affirmation of life, with a *"Welt-Bejahung,"* the Protestant, should now, with minor exceptions, have fallen into a denial of life, a fear of animal "robustiousness," while the other group, which persistently belittled this life and lived in the shadow of immortality, should be exhibiting in our day every evidence of that affirmation which Protestantism once made.   Protestantism as a traditional way of life has got too far away from nature.   Sophistication has been too much for it. Given our present attitude to life, we are probably fighting our last victorious war.   If the test comes again in the future, we shall have too few young men to fend off the races such as the Japanese that ask less return from life but are more able to live.   Our people are willing to make every effort to ensure by military means the immediate survival of their group but they seem not to have the slightest interest in what may happen to it a few years into the future.   It may therefore be that their fate, too, is to

---

[18]CHILDREN 0-4 YEARS OF AGE PER 1,000 OF TOTAL

Denomination	Children 0-4 per 1,000 of total
Mennonites	159.3
Roman Catholics	125.5
Mormons	123.3
Greek Orthodox	121.7
Pentecostals	103.7
Lutherans	97.8
Baptists	90.5
United Church	87.5
Anglicans	85.5
Presbyterians	80.5
Salvation Army	75.5
Jews	75.0
Christian Science	45.3

Table compiled from 1931 census, vol. III, p. 310.

pass under the harrow and from intimate contemplation of the arrogant superior, find for themselves the secret that the humble already know. *Deposuit magnifices de sedibus.* . . .

Does this mean that we shall have to choose between the way of life we have built up and our survival as a group? Shall we have to return to what most of us would feel to be a much poorer kind of civilization? I trust not, though if our civilization is to survive I am certain that some kind of compromise will have to be effected and many aspects of our present way of life greatly modified. Amid much that is good many of them are just idiotic. Everyone can amuse himself by compiling his own list of lunacies, but conspicuous among the major changes that will have to come is a modification of the ethic of acquisition, the *appetitus divitiarum infinitus,* the unbridled indulgence of the acquisitive appetite, as Tawney puts it and the degenerate indulgence that surely accompanies it.

If our urban civilization were to fall through dry rot, through failure of man-power, hardly less ironical a fate would be in store for the non-acquisitive group, which is, in Canada, the French. Without the initiative of the English Protestant man of business, the present-day mechanical civilization could not have come into existence. Without it, the French would have remained a quiet rural people, probably not more than a quarter as numerous as they are now. If old William Price, or some other, had not opened up the Saguenay a century and a quarter ago, and if his successors had not built on to his achievements, instead of the lumber, the pulpwood, the water-power and the aluminum that now come out of that valley, there would have been a few farms on the shores of Lake St. John, a few small local saw-mills, and that would have been all. There would have been that many fewer opportunities for life. The industrial structure of Quebec rests on this initiative, which has provided work for the hundreds of thousands from the countryside who otherwise would have had to stay on the farm as bachelors and spinsters, or divide and subdivide the land in Malthusian misery. The question forces itself, "who has created the French race in America?" I make bold to say that the English industrialist has created about three-quarters of it.[14]

So the fate of the two peoples seems indissolubly linked. At present they complement each other, unhappily and acrimoniously. But may the day not come when understanding will be greater? May the English not learn a little tolerance, the French gain a little breadth? May the English, through suffering, perhaps, lose a little of their arrogance, the French a little of their touchy vanity? May the extreme commercialism of the English not be modified, the more obvious blatancies of their civilization overcome, their acquisitive ethic toned down? May the French not come forward and take their place in running a modern state, finding constructive ideas to contribute, getting a little further away from medievalism, from a philosophy that sacrifices nearly everything to survival value? May the deep fear which afflicts both sides—the fear of the French of losing their identity and the fear of the English of being outnumbered—not be dissipated in a common loyalty to a common country?

That day may come and it may not. Pressure from the outside world may bring it, though of that I am doubtful. The lessening numbers of the English may induce in them more of a live-and-let-live attitude. The

---

[14]Reckoning in the industrial French population of the United States.

penetrative qualities of North American civilization may bring French society closer to the continental norm. Most likely of all, it seems to me, the tensions and troubles of our times, which are not going to end with the peace, will some day burn out the grosser aspects of our English materialism, giving us a truer and deeper insight into life than what we have now, reforming our society in some such way as society was reshaped at the end of the middle ages and thereby establishing a new set of values in which both races can share. The two communities will never be one, there can be no question of a blood brotherhood, but sooner or later they will take up their respective weights, some kind of equilibrium will be reached, of that I am sure. We have not lived together for nearly two centuries merely to see the Canadian experiment fail. It will not fail. This country of high colours and violent contrasts will not fail. One of these days the two races, forgetting lesser allegiances, will unite in mutual loyalty to it, and build it into a structure of which our successors will be proud.

Some Reflections on the
Liberal Tradition in Canada

FRANK H. UNDERHILL

"THE reader is about to enter upon the most violent and certainly the most eventful moral struggle that has ever taken place in our North American colonies. . . . That I was sentenced to contend on the soil of America with Democracy, and that if I did not overpower it, it would overpower me, were solemn facts which for some weeks had been perfectly evident to my mind." So wrote Sir Francis Bond Head in his *Narrative*,[1] the famous apologia for the policy of his governorship of Upper Canada. The issue as he saw it, and as his contemporaries in Canada saw it, was not merely whether the British North American colonies were to set up a responsible form of government; it was the much deeper one of whether they were to follow the example of the United States and commit themselves to achieving a democratic form of society. And good Sir Francis appealed with confidence to all right-thinking property-owning Englishmen against what he termed "the insane theory of conciliating democracy" as put into practice by the Colonial Office under the guidance of that "rank republican," Mr. Under-Secretary Stephen. No doubt, if the phrase had been then in use he would have accused Stephen, and Lord Glenelg and Lord Durham, of appeasement. In rebuttal of Durham's criticisms of the Upper Canada Family Compact he wrote:

> It appears from Lord Durham's own showing that this "Family Compact" which his Lordship deems it so advisable that the Queen should destroy, is nothing more nor less than that "social fabric" which characterizes every civilized community in the world. . . . "The bench," "the magistrates," "the clergy," "the law," "the landed proprietors," "the bankers," "the native-born inhabitants," and "the supporters of the Established Church" [these were the social groups which Durham had defined as composing the Family Compact] form just as much "*a family compact*" in England as they do in Upper Canada, and just as much in Germany as they do in England. . . . The "*family compact*" of Upper Canada is composed of those members of its society who, either by their abilities and character, have been honoured by the confidence of the executive government, or who by their industry and intelligence, have amassed wealth. The party, I own, is comparatively a small one; but to put the multitude at the top and the few at the bottom is a radical reversion of the pyramid of society which every reflecting man must foresee can end only by its downfall.[2]

Sir Francis's statement is as clear and as trenchant an enunciation of the anti-democratic conservative political philosophy of his day as could be quoted from the American conservatives who were fighting Jacksonian Democracy at this same time or from the English conservatives who were fighting the Reform Bill or Chartism. As we all know, this "moral struggle" over the

---

[1] Sir Francis Bond Head, *A Narrative* (London, 1839), 64.
[2] *Ibid.*, 464.

Reprinted from Canadian Historical Association, *Report*, 1946

fundamental principles on which society should be based, which Sir Francis correctly discerned as representing the real meaning of the Canadian party strife of the eighteen-thirties, was to be decided against him and his tory friends. The century since his *Narrative* was published has been, in the English-speaking world at least, a period of continuously developing liberal and democratic movements. Liberalism has merged into democracy. Today the people of Canada are recovering from the second world war within a generation in defence of democracy. Presumably, considering the sacrifices we have shown ourselves willing to make for the cause, we Canadians cherish passionately the liberal-democratic tradition which is our inheritance from the nineteenth century. Presumably, the growth of liberal-democratic institutions and ideas in our political, economic, and social life is one of the main themes in our Canadian history, just as it certainly is in the history of Great Britain and the United States, the two communities with which we have most intimately shared our experience.

Yet it is a remarkable fact that in the great debate of our generation, the debate which has been going on all over the Western World about the fundamental values of liberalism and democracy, we Canadians have taken very little part. We talk at length of the status which our nation has attained in the world. We have shown in two great wars that we can produce soldiers and airmen and sailors second to none. We have organized our productive resources so energetically as to make ourselves one of the main arsenals and granaries of democracy. We have achieved political autonomy and economic maturity. But to the discussion of those deep underlying intellectual, moral and spiritual issues which have made such chaos of the contemporary world we Canadians are making very little contribution.

Our Confederation was achieved at the very time in the nineteenth century when a reaction was beginning to set in against the liberal and democratic principles which, springing from eighteenth-century Enlightenment, had seemed up to that moment to be winning ever fresh victories. The liberal nationalism of the early part of the century was beginning to turn into something sinister, the passionate, exclusive, irrational, totalitarian nationalism that we know today. The optimistic belief in human equality and perfectibility was beginning to be undermined by new knowledge about man provided by the researches of biologists and psychologists. At the same time technological developments in mass production industries were building up a new social pyramid with a few owners and managers at the top and the mass of exploited workers at the bottom; and new techniques of mass propaganda still further emphasized this division of mankind into *élite* and masses. The freedom which our Victorian ancestors thought was slowly broadening down from precedent to precedent seemed to become more and more unreal under the concentrated pressure of capitalistic big business or of the massive bureaucratic state. In such surroundings, the liberal spirit does not flourish. And the more reflective minds of our day have been acutely aware that the mere winning of military victories under banners labelled "liberty" or "democracy" does not carry us very far in the solving of our deeper problems.

Canada is caught up in this modern crisis of liberalism as are all other national communities. But in this world-debate about the values of our civilization the Canadian voice is hardly heard. Who ever reads a Canadian book? What Canadian books are there on these problems? What have we had to say about them that has attracted the attention of our contemporaries or has impressed itself upon their imagination? In the world of ideas we do not yet play a full part. We are still colonial. Our thinking is still derivative. Like other peoples Canadians have of late expended a good deal of misdirected energy in endeavours to export goods without importing other goods in return. But we continue to import ideas without trying to develop an export trade in this field. We are in fact, as I have said, colonial. For our intellectual capital we are still dependent upon a continuous flow of imports from London, New York, and Paris, not to mention Moscow and Rome. It is to be hoped that we will continue to raise our intellectual standards by continuing to import from these more mature centres, and that we will never try to go in for intellectual autarchy. But international commerce in ideas as well as in goods should be a two-way traffic at least, and preferably it should be multilateral.

Incidentally, it is worth remarking in passing that one sign of this colonialism in our intellectual world is to be seen in the present state of Canadian historiography. The guild of Canadian historians confine their activities very largely to the writing of studies in local national history. South of the border American historians have long been demonstrating their intellectual equality by pouring out books on English and European and world history as well as on local subjects. But how little of this kind of research and writing has been done in Canada! During the past year we have lost one of our most distinguished colleagues, in the person of Professor Charles Norris Cochrane; and his book on *Christianity and Classical Culture* is a notable example of the sort of thing I mean. But one cannot think of many cases like this, in which we have asserted our full partnership in the civilization of our day by Canadian writing upon the great subjects of permanent and universal interest.

* * *

Now it seems to me—and this is more or less the main theme of the present rambling discursive paper—that this intellectual weakness of Canada is a quality which shows itself through all our history. In particular it is to be discerned in that process of democratization which is the most important thing that has happened to us, as to other kindred peoples, during the last hundred years. When we compare ourselves with Britain and the United States there is one striking contrast. Those two countries, since the end of the eighteenth century, have abounded in prophets and philosophers who have made articulate the idea of a liberal and equalitarian society. Their political history displays also a succession of practical politicians who have not merely performed the functions of manipulating and manoeuvring masses of men and groups which every politician performs, but whose careers have struck the imagination of both contemporaries and descendants as symbolizing certain great inspiring ideas. We in Canada have produced few such figures. Where are the classics in our political literature which embody our Canadian version of liberalism and democracy? Our party struggles have never been raised to the higher intellectual plane at which they become of universal interest by the presence of a Canadian Jefferson and a Canadian Hamilton in opposing parties. We have had no Canadian Burke or Mill to perform the social function of the political philosopher in action. We have had no Canadian Carlyle or Ruskin or Arnold to ask searching questions about the ultimate values embodied in our political or economic practice. We lack a Canadian Walt Whitman or Mark Twain to give literary expression to the democratic way of life. The student in search of illustrative material on the growth of Canadian political ideas during the great century of liberalism and democracy has to content himself mainly with a collection of extracts from more or less forgotten speeches and pamphlets and newspaper editorials. Whatever urge may have, at any time, possessed any Canadian to philosophize upon politics did not lead to much writing whose intrinsic worth helped to preserve it in our memory.

At least this is true of us English-speaking Canadians. Our French-speaking fellow citizens have shown a much greater fondness and capacity for ideas in politics than we have; but their writings, being in another language, have hardly penetrated into our English-Canadian consciousness.

We early repudiated the philosophy of the Manchester School; but in the long history of our Canadian "National Policy" it is difficult to find any Canadian exposition of the anti-Manchester ideas of a national economy, written by economist, business man, or politician, which has impressed itself upon us as worthy of preservation. Our history is full of agrarian protest movements, but the ordinary Canadian would be stumped if asked to name any representative Canadian philosopher of agrarianism. And the most notable illustration of this poverty of our politics at the intellectual level is to be found in the fact that while we were the pioneers in one of the great liberal achievements of the nineteenth century—the experiment of responsible government, which transformed the British Empire into the Commonwealth, and which has thrown fresh light in our own day on the possibility of reconciling nationalism with a wider international community—even in this field, in which our practical contribution was so great, there has arisen since the days of Joseph Howe no Canadian prophet of the idea of the Commonwealth whose writings seem inspiring or even readable to wider circles than those of professional historians.

This seeming incapacity for ideas, or rather this habit of carrying on our communal affairs at a level at which ideas never quite emerge into an articulate life of their own, has surely impoverished our Canadian politics. Every teacher of Canadian history has this fact brought home to him with each fresh batch of young students whom he meets. How reluctant they are to study the history of their own country! How eagerly they show their preference for English or European or (if they get the chance) for American history! For they instinctively feel that when they get outside of Canada they are studying the great creative seminal ideas that have determined the character of our modern world, whereas inside Canada there seem to be no ideas at issue of permanent or universal significance at all. I can myself still remember the thrill of appreciation with which as a university freshman I heard a famous professor of Greek[3] remark that our Canadian history is as dull as ditchwater, and our politics is full of it. Of course there is a considerable amount of ditchwater in the politics of all countries; my professor was more conscious of it in Canada because he missed here those ideas which he found in the politics of classical Greece. And as far as I have been able to observe, young students of this present generation are still repelled by

---

[3]Maurice Hutton, Principal of University College in the University of Toronto.

Canadian history because they find in it little more than the story of a half-continent of material resources over which a population of some twelve million economic animals have spread themselves in a not too successful search for economic wealth.

*   *   *

It will of course be said in answer to these mournful reflections upon the low quality of intellectual activity in Canadian politics that they are exaggerated and extreme.   So I should like to buttress my position by referring to observations made at different times by students from the outer world upon the nature and quality of Canadian party politics. The name of Goldwin Smith[4]comes to mind at once.   He watched and studied Canadian politics continuously from the early eighteen-seventies to the early nineteen-hundreds, applying to them the standards of an English Manchester liberal; and his verdict was adverse.   He felt that Canadians after 1867 had failed to rise to their intellectual opportunities, that they had failed to grasp in their imagination the potentialities of the new nationality, that their political parties operated only to debase and pervert the discussion of public issues, and that in the absence of great guiding inspiring ideas Canadian national statesmanship had degenerated into a sordid business of bargaining and manoeuvring among narrow selfish particularist interest groups.   He took a certain sardonic pleasure in noting the skill with which Macdonald played this low game as contrasted with the clumsiness with which Mackenzie and Blake played it; but he could see in it nothing but a low game after all. The obvious reply to Goldwin Smith is that he was embittered by the disappointment of his own ambitions and that his testimony is therefore to be discounted. But no one who studies the politics of the period 1867 to 1914 can be convinced that this is a wholly satisfactory defence against his criticisms.

At the period of the turn of the century, we were studied by another overseas observer who has given us the most penetrating and illuminating analysis of our politics that has yet been written by anyone, native or foreign.   In 1906 André Siegfried published his book, *The Race Question in Canada,* and set forth the somewhat paradoxical conclusion that, while (to quote his opening sentence) "Canadian politics are a tilting ground for impassioned rivalries," they operated so as to suppress the intellectual vitality which would be the natural result of such a situation.

> Originally formed to subserve a political idea, these parties are often to be found quite detached from the principles which gave them birth, and with their own self-preservation as their chief care and aim.   Even without a programme, they continue to live and thrive, tending to become mere associations for the securing of power; their doctrines serving merely as weapons, dulled or sharpened, grasped as occasion arises for use in the fight. . . . This fact deprives the periodical appeals to the voting public of the importance which they should have. . . . Whichever side succeeds, the country it is well known will be governed in just the same way; the only difference will be in the *personnel* of the Government. That is how things go save when some great wave of feeling sweeps over the Dominion, submerging all the pigmies of politics in its flood.

---

[4]See F. H. Underhill, "Goldwin Smith" (*University of Toronto Quarterly,* II, Apr., 1933).

In the intervals between these crises.... it is not the party that subserves the idea, it is the idea that subserves the party. Canadian statesmen...undoubtedly take longer views. They seem, however, to stand
in fear of great movements of public opinion, and to seek to lull them
rather than to encourage them and bring them to fruition. Thus, deliberately and not from short-sightedness, they help to promote the state
of things which I have described. The reason for this attitude is easy
to comprehend. Canada, with its rival creeds and races, is a land of
fears and jealousies and conflicts.... Let a question involving religion
or nationality be once boldly raised... and the elections will be turned
into real political fights, passionate and sincere. This is exactly what
is dreaded by far-sighted and prudent politicians, whose duty it is to
preserve the national equilibrium.... They exert themselves, therefore,
to prevent the formation of homogeneous parties, divided according
to creed or race or class. The purity of political life suffers from this,
but perhaps the very existence of the Federation is the price. The
existing parties are thus entirely harmless. The Liberals and Conservatives differ very little really in their opinions upon crucial questions, and
their views as to administration are almost identical.... They have come
to regard each other without alarm: they know each other too well and
resemble each other too closely.[5]

Mr. J. A. Hobson, the well-known English economist, published a little
book about Canada at almost the same moment as M. Siegfried—*Canada Today,* which appeared in 1906. It also gives a rather unfavourable impression
of Canadian politics, although the author's main interest was in the economic
question of protection and the British preference.

More recently another great student of politics from overseas has given
us his observations upon Canada. James Bryce had played an active part
in the politics of his own country, had made himself intimately acquainted
with the American Commonwealth, and applied to Canada a mind that was
deeply learned in comparative politics. In his book, *Modern Democracies,*
published in 1921, he devoted some chapters to the working of Canadian
democracy.

Since 1867 the questions which have had the most constant interest
for the bulk of the nation are . . . those which belong to the sphere of
commercial and industrial progress, the development of the material
resources of the country . . . —matters scarcely falling within the lines
by which party opinion is divided, for the policy of *laissez faire* has few
adherents in a country which finds in governmental action or financial
support to private enterprises the quickest means of carrying out every
promising project. . . . The task of each party is to persuade the people
that in this instance its plan promises quicker and larger results, and that
it is fitter to be trusted with the work. Thus it happens that general
political principles . . . count for little in politics, though ancient habit
requires them to be invoked. Each party tries to adapt itself from time
to time to whatever practical issue may arise. Opportunism is inevitable,
and the charge of inconsistency, though incessantly bandied to and fro,
is lightly regarded. . . . In Canada ideas are not needed to make parties,

[5]André Siegfried, *The Race Question in Canada* (English translation, London,
1907), 141-3.

for these can live by heredity. . . . The people show an abounding party spirit when an election day arrives. The constant party struggle keeps their interest alive. But party spirit, so far from being a measure of the volume of political thinking, may even be a substitute for thinking. . . . In every country a game played over material interests between ministers, constituencies and their representatives, railway companies and private speculators is not only demoralizing to all concerned but interferes with the consideration of the great issues of policy on a wise handling of which a nation's welfare depends. Fiscal questions, labour questions, the assumption by the State of such branches of industry as railroads or mines, and the principles it ought to follow in such works as it under-takes—questions like these need wide vision, clear insight, and a firmness that will resist political pressure and adhere to the principles once laid down. These qualities have been wanting, and the people have begun to perceive the want.[6]

* * *

This general failure of our Canadian politics to rise above a mere confused struggle of interest groups has been no doubt due to a variety of causes. In the middle of the twentieth century it is rather too late for us to keep harping on the pioneer frontier character of the Canadian community as the all sufficient answer to criticism. The young American republic which included a Jefferson and a Hamilton and a Franklin, not to mention many of their contemporaries of almost equal intellectual stature, was a smaller and more isolated frontier community than Canada has been for a long time; but it was already by the end of the eighteenth century the peer of Europe in the quality of its political thinking and was recognized as such. We still remain colonial in the middle of the twentieth century.

One reason for our backwardness, and the reason which interests me most at the moment, has been the weakness of the Radical and Reform parties of the Left in our Canadian history. A healthy society will consist of a great majority massed a little to the right and a little to the left of centre, with smaller groups of strong conservatives and strong radicals out on the wings. If these minority groups are not present in any significant force to provide a perpetual challenge to the majority, the conservatives and liberals of the centre are likely to be a pretty flabby lot, both intellectually and morally.

For this weakness of the Left in Canada, the ultimate explanation would seem to be that we never had an eighteenth century of our own. The intellectual life of our politics has not been periodically revived by fresh drafts from the invigorating fountain of eighteenth-century Enlightenment. In Catholic French Canada the doctrines of the rights of man and of Liberty Equality Fraternity were rejected from the start, and to this day they have never penetrated, save surreptitiously or spasmodically. The mental climate of English Canada in its early formative years was determined by men who were fleeing from the practical application of the doctrines that all men are born equal and are endowed by their Creator with certain unalienable rights among which are life liberty and the pursuit of happiness. All effective liberal and radical democratic movements in the nineteenth century have had their roots in this fertile eighteenth-century soil. But our ancestors made the great refusal

---

[6]James Bryce, *Modern Democracies* (New York, 1921), I, 471-505. Bryce's ana-lysis was based mainly upon observations made before World War I.

in the eighteenth century. In Canada we have no revolutionary tradition; and our historians, political scientists, and philosophers have assiduously tried to educate us to be proud of this fact. How can such a people expect their democracy to be dynamic as the democracies of Britain and France and the United States have been?

Then also it has never been sufficiently emphasized that our first great democratic upheaval a hundred years ago was a failure. In the United States, Jacksonian Democracy swept away most of the old aristocratic survivals and made a strong attack upon the new plutocratic forces. The Federalists disappeared; and their successors, the Whigs, suffered a series of defeats at the hands of triumphant Democracy. But the Canadian version of Jacksonian Democracy represented by the movements of Papineau and Mackenzie was discredited by the events of their abortive rebellions. And Canada followed the example of Britain rather than of the United States. Responsible government was a British technique of government which took the place of American elective institutions. Our historians have been so dazzled by its success that they have failed to point out that the real radicals in Canada were pushed aside in the eighteen-forties by the respectable professional and property-owning classes, the "Moderates" as we call them; just as the working-class radicals in Britain, without whose mass-agitation the Reform Bill could not have been passed, were pushed aside after 1832 for a long generation of middle class Whig rule. The social pyramid in Canada about which Sir Francis Bond Head was so worried in 1839 was *not* upset; and after a decade of excitement it was clear that the Reform government was only a business men's government. When Baldwin and Lafontaine were succeeded by Hincks and Morin this was so clear that new radical movements emerged both in Upper and in Lower Canada, the Grits and les Rouges,

Now in North America the essence of all effective liberal movements—I assume in this paper that liberalism naturally leads towards democracy—must be that they are attacks upon the domination of the community by the business man. This was what the Democratic party of Jackson and Van Buren was. As Mr. Schlesinger has recently been pointing out in his brilliant book, *The Age of Jackson,*[7] the effectiveness of the Jacksonians was due to the fact that their leading ideas about the relations of business and government came primarily not from the frontier farmers of the west but from the democratic labour movements in the big cities and their sympathizers among the urban intellectuals. Jefferson had been mainly interested in political democracy; Jackson tackled the problem of economic democracy in a society becoming increasingly industrialized. The social equality of the frontier has never given agrarian democrats a sufficient understanding of the problems of a society divided into the rich and the poor of an urban civilization. Here we seem to come upon an important explanation for the weakness of all Canadian radical movements from the eighteen-thirties to the end of the century. They were too purely agrarian. The only force that could ultimately overcome the Hamiltonians must, like them, have its base of operations in the cities.

Mr. Schlesinger has also pointed out that American conservatism was immensely strengthened when it transformed itself from Federalism to Whiggism. In the eighteen-thirties, as he puts it, it changed from broadcloth to homespun. "The metamorphosis revived it politically but ruined it intel-

---

[7]A. M. Schlesinger, Jr., *The Age of Jackson* (Boston, 1945).

lectually. The Federalists had thought about society in an intelligent and hard-boiled way. The Whigs, in scuttling Federalism, replaced it by a social philosophy founded, not on ideas, but on subterfuges and sentimentalities."[8] But the Whigs learned the techniques of demagogy from the Jacksonians and set out to guide the turbulent new American democracy along lines that would suit the purposes of business. Surely we should remark that exactly the same metamorphosis took place just a little later in Canadian conservatism. The clear-cut anti-democratic philosophy of Sir Francis Bond Head and the Family Compact Tories was as obsolete and out-of-place in the bustling Canada of the eighteen-fifties as Federalism had been in the United States in the eighteen-twenties. The Macdonald-Cartier Liberal-Conservative party was American Whiggism with a British title. (And no doubt the British label on the outside added considerably to the potency of the American liquor inside the bottle.) The Liberal-Conservatives had made the necessary demagogic adjustments to the democratic spirit of the times; they had a policy of economic expansion to be carried out under the leadership of business with the assistance of government which was an almost exact parallel to Clay's Whig "American System." But there was no Jackson and no Jacksonian "kitchen cabinet" in Canada to counter this Liberal-Conservatism.

The Grits and les Rouges did not quite meet the needs of the situation. What Rougeism, with its body of ideas from the revolutionary Paris of 1848, might have accomplished we cannot say; for it soon withered under the onslaught of the Church. Grittism in Upper Canada was originally a movement inspired by American ideas, as its early fondness for elective institutions and its continuing insistence on "Rep by Pop" show. But Brown's accession tended to shift the inspiration in the British direction. Brown himself became more and more sentimentally British as he grew older. Moreover, as publisher of the *Globe*, he was a business man on the make, and Toronto was a growing business centre. As Toronto grew, and as the *Globe* grew, the original frontier agrarianism of the Grits was imperceptibly changed into something subtly different. As early as January 3, 1857 the *Globe* was declaring: "The schemes of those who have announced that Toronto must aspire no higher than to be 'the Capital of an agricultural District' must be vigorously met and overcome." Brown defeated the radicals from the Peninsula in the great Reform convention of 1859, and by 1867 Grit leaders were more and more becoming urban business and professional men. A party which contained William McMaster of the Bank of Commerce and John Macdonald, the big wholesale merchant, was not likely to be very radical. Oliver Mowat, a shrewd cautious lawyer, was about to take over the direction of its forces in Ontario provincial politics; and its rising hope in the federal sphere was Edward Blake, the leader of the Ontario equity bar. Moreover, as Brown's unhappy experiences with his printers in 1872 were to show, the Reform party under *Globe* inspiration found difficulty in adjusting itself to the new ideas which industrialism was encouraging in the minds of the working class. Blake and Mowat, who dominated Canadian Liberal thinking after Brown, were not American democrats or radicals so much as English Whigs in their temperament, their training, and their political philosophy. For political equality and liberty they were

[8]*Ibid.*, 279.

prepared to fight; economic equality did not move them very deeply. And the same might be said about Laurier who succeeded them.[9]

Another point worth noting is the effect of British influences in slowing down all movements throughout the nineteenth century in the direction of the democratization of politics and society. Inevitably, because of geographical proximity and the mutual interpenetration of the lives of the two North American communities, the urge towards greater democracy was likely to appear in Canada as an American influence; and since the survival of Canada as a separate entity depended on her not being submerged under an American flood, such influences were fought as dangerous to our Canadian ethos. Sir Francis Bond Head and the Tories of his time habitually used the words "democratic" and "republican" as interchangeable. Every Canadian movement of the Left in those days and since has had to meet accusations of Americanism, and in proving its sound British patriotism it has been apt to lose a good deal of its Leftism. Canadian Methodism, for example, widely influenced by its American connections, was on the Reform side of politics until the Ryerson arrangement in the eighteen-thirties with the British Wesleyans put it on the other side.

When we get down to the Confederation period no one can fail to see how markedly the British influence gives a conservative tone to the whole generation of the Fathers. Later Canadians have had to reflect frequently on the sad fact that the "new nationality" was very imperfectly based upon any deep popular feeling. It has occurred to many of them, with the wisdom of hindsight, that Confederation would have been a much stronger structure had the Quebec Resolutions received the ratification of the electorate in each colony in accordance with American precedents. But the British doctrine of legislative sovereignty operated to override all suggestions that the people should be consulted; and Canadian nationality has always been weak in its moral appeal because "We the People" had no formal part in bringing it into being.

Similarly British example was effective in delaying the arrival of manhood suffrage in Canada till toward the end of the century, though the Americans had adopted it in the early part of the century. The ballot did not become part of Canadian law until sanctioned by British precedent in the eighteen-seventies. .The Chancery Court which had long been a favourite object of radical attack in Upper Canada remained intact until jurists of the Mother Country had amalgamated the equity and common law jurisdictions there. And that strange constitutional device, the Canadian Senate, with its life appointees, was slipped into our constitution with the plea that appointment by the Crown

[9]On the Liberal party see further F. H. Underhill's articles on:
(1) "Some Aspects of Upper Canadian Political Opinion in the Decade before Confederation" (*Canadian Historical Association Report*, 1927).
(2) "Canada's Relations with the Empire as seen by the Toronto *Globe*, 1857-67" (*Canadian Historical Review*, XX, June, 1929).
(3) "The Development of National Political Parties in Canada" (*Canadian Historical Review*, XVI, Dec., 1935).
(4) "Edward Blake, the Liberal Party and Unrestricted Reciprocity" (*Canadian Historical Association Report*, 1939).
(5) "Edward Blake and Canadian Liberal Nationalism" (in R. Flenley, *Essays in Canadian History*, Toronto, 1939).
(6) "Political Ideas of the Upper Canada Reformers, 1867-78" (*Canadian Historical Association Report*, 1942).
(7) "The Canadian Party System in Transition" (*Canadian Journal of Economics and Political Science*, IX, Aug., 1943).

was the British way of doing things.   John A. Macdonald must have had his tongue in his cheek when he presented this Senate as a protector of provincial rights, its members being appointed by the head of the very federal government against which provincial rights were to be protected.   In the privacy of the Quebec Conference, when they were constructing the second chamber, he had remarked to his fellow delegates: "The rights of the minority must be protected, and the rich are always fewer in number than the poor."   One wonders what George Brown or Oliver Mowat, the Grit representatives, must have said at this point, or whether the secretary, who caught Macdonald's immortal sentence, failed to take down their comments.   Generally speaking, the notable fact is that in all this era of constitution making, and of constitution testing in the decades just after 1867, the voice of democratic radicalism was so weak.

On the other hand, when Britain began to grow really democratic towards the end of the nineteenth century, her example seemed to have little effect upon Canadian liberalism.   The two most significant features in internal British politics since the eighteen-eighties have been the rise of industrial labour to a share of power both in the economic and in the political field, and the growing tendency towards collectivism in social policy.   We are only beginning to enter upon this stage of development in Canada today.   Throughout it has been the conservative trends in English life that we have usually copied.   And one of the few sources of innocent amusement left in the present tortured world is to watch the growing embarrassment of all those professional exponents in Canada of the English way of doing things, now that the English way threatens to become less conservative.

* * *

Of course the great force, by far the most important force, weakening liberal and democratic tendencies in Canada after 1867 was the rush to exploit the resources of a rich half continent.   This was the age in American history which Parrington has called "The Great Barbecue."

> The spirit of the frontier was to flare up in a huge buccaneering orgy.... Congress had rich gifts to bestow—in lands, tariffs, subsidies, favors of all sorts; and when influential citizens had made their wishes known to the reigning statesmen, the sympathetic politicians were quick to turn the government into the fairy godmother the voters wanted it to be. A huge barbecue was spread to which all presumably were invited. Not quite all, to be sure; inconspicuous persons, those who were at home on the farm or at work in the mills and offices were overlooked.... But all the important people, leading bankers and promoters and business men, received invitations.... To a frontier people what was more democratic than a barbecue, and to a paternal age what was more fitting than that the state should provide the beeves for roasting? Let all come and help themselves.... But unfortunately what was intended to be jovially democratic was marred by displays of plebeian temper. Suspicious commoners with better eyes than manners discovered the favoritism of the waiters, and drew attention to their own meager helpings and the heaped-up plates of the more favored guests.[10]

[10]Vernon Louis Parrington, *Main Currents in American Thought,* Volume III, *The Beginnings of Critical Realism in America* (New York, 1930), 23.

Parrington's description fits the Canadian situation also, though our bar-becue did not get going in full force till after 1896. In the first generation after Confederation, Canadian Liberals wandered mostly in the deserts of opposition because they could not produce any policy which could match in attractiveness the economic expansionism of the Conservatives. They criti-cized the extravagant pace of Conservative policy, they denounced the cor-ruption of the Macdonald system, they pointed with true prophecy to the danger of building up great business corporations like the C.P.R. which might become more powerful than the national government itself. But the spirit of the Great Barbecue was too strong for them. And when finally they did come into office under Laurier they gave up the struggle. The effort to control this social force of the business-man-on-the-make was abandoned. Their moral abhorrence of the methods of Macdonald gave place with a striking rapidity to an ever deepening cynicism. "You say we should at once set to reform the tariff," Laurier wrote to his chief journalistic supporter after the victory of 1896, "This I consider impossible except after ample discus-sion with the business men." And until he made the fatal mistake of reciprocity in 1911, the Liberal government was conducted on the basis of ample dis-cussion with the business men.

It is easy to say that this was inevitable in the circumstances of the time. And indeed the remarkable fact about the Canada of the turn of the century is the slowness of other social groups in acquiring political consciousness and organizing movements of revolt against government by business men. Ameri-can populism was only faintly reflected amongst Canadian farmers until the nineteen-twenties. The Progressive movement which helped to bring Theodore Roosevelt and Woodrow Wilson to the White House seemed to cause few repercussions north of the border. Everybody in Canada in those days was reading the popular American magazines as they carried on the spectacular campaigns of the muckraking era against the trusts. But this fierce attack next door to us against the domination of society by big business stirred few echoes in Canadian public life. Our Canadian millionaires continued to die in the odour of sanctity. Canadian liberalism in the Laurier era was equally little affected by the contemporary transformation of the British Liberal party into a great radical social-reform movement.

What seems especially to have struck visitors from across the ocean was the absence of any effective labour movement in Canadian politics. Both André Siegfried from France and J. A. Hobson from England remarked upon this phenomenon in the books which they published in 1906. "When the workers of Canada wake up," said Hobson, "they will find that Protection is only one among the several economic fangs fastened in their 'corpus vile' by the little group of railroad men, bankers, lumber men and manufacturing monopolists who own their country."[11]

The Great Barbecue was still in full swing when these observers studied Canada. As I have said already, liberalism in North America, if it is to mean anything concrete, must mean an attack upon the domination of institu-tions and ideas by the business man. In this sense Canadian liberalism re-vived after 1918, to produce results with which we are all familiar. Among those results, however, we can hardly include any advance in the clarity or the realism of the liberal thinking of the so-called Liberal party, however

---

[11] J. A. Hobson, *Canada Today* (London, 1906), 47.

much we may be compelled to admire its dexterity in the practical arts of maintaining itself in office. In the realm of political ideas its performance may be correctly described as that of going on and on and on, and up and up and up. But I am now touching upon present-day controversies. And, whatever latitude may be allowed to the political scientist, we all know that the historian cannot deal with current events without soiling the purity of his scientific objectivity.

* * *

In the meantime Canadian historians must continue to study and to write the history of their country. I have devoted these rambling remarks to the subject of political ideas because I have a feeling that Canadian historiography has come to the end of an epoch. For the past twenty or thirty years, most of the best work in Canadian history has been in the economic field. How different groups of Canadians made their living, how a national economy was built up, how the Canadian economy was integrated into a world economy, these topics have been industriously investigated; and we have been given thereby a new and a deeper understanding of the basis of our national life. The climax in this school of activity was reached with the publication of the Carnegie series on Canadian-American relations and of the various volumes connected with the Rowell-Sirois Report.

The best work in the Carnegie collection is for the most part on the economic side. And the volume, published during the past year, which crowns the series—Professor Bartlet Brebner's *North American Triangle*—can hardly be praised too highly for the skill and insight with which the author brings out the pattern of the joint Canadian-American achievement in settling the continent and exploiting its economic resources, and with which he explains the practical working of our peculiar North American techniques and forms of organization. But it is significant that he has little to say about the intellectual history of the two peoples, about education, religion, and such subjects; and especially about the idea of democracy as understood in North America. Materials from research on the intellectual history of Canada were not, as a matter of fact, available to him in any quantity. Volume I of the Rowell-Sirois Report is likewise a brilliant and, within its field, a convincing exercise in the economic interpretation of Canadian history. But it is abstract history without names or real flesh-and-blood individuals, the history of puppets who dance on strings pulled by obscure world forces which they can neither understand nor control; it presents us with a ghostly ballet of bloodless economic categories.

The time seems about due for a new history-writing which will attempt to explain the ideas in the heads of Canadians that caused them to act as they did, their philosophy, why they thought in one way at one period and in a different way at another period. Perhaps when we settle down to this task we shall discover that our ancestors had more ideas in their heads than this paper has been willing to concede them. At any rate, we shall then be able to understand more clearly the place of the Canadian people in the civilization of the liberal-democratic century which lies behind us.

Clio in Canada:
The Interpretation of Canadian History

W. L. MORTON

IN Canada much effort has now been given to historical research. Much less attention, to all appearances, has been devoted to problems of historical criticism, particularly to those which arise when the field of reference is narrowed down to that of national history. Yet certain well-defined interpretations of Canadian history have been developed, and have shaped historical thought in Canada and popular understanding of Canadian history. This paper intends no more than to raise the questions: upon what critical premises have these interpretations been raised, and what has been their effect in terms of historical thinking and popular knowledge?

Criticism implies standards, and standards imply function. It is submitted that the standards of historical criticism are in the long run empiric, the historian's knowledge of his subject and, to a varying lesser degree, of his times and his fellow men. In Professor Barzun's words: "the worth of history consists . . . in the diagnostic power that it develops."[1] The function of historical study is to put questions to ascertainable relics of the past. As R. G. Collingwood remarks:

Each question and each answer in a given complex [has] to be relevant or appropriate, [has] to 'belong' both to the whole and to the place it [occupies] in the whole. Each question [has] to 'arise'; there must be that about it whose absence we condemn when we refuse to answer a question on the ground that it 'doesn't arise.' Each answer must be the 'right' answer to the question it professes to answer.

By 'right' I do not mean 'true.' The 'right' answer to a question is the answer which enables us to get ahead with the process of questioning and answering.[2]

But what determines the questions the historian puts? He puts a question because he wants an answer, not a particular answer to a question, but an answer to a particular question. That question is determined by his interest in it, the interest arising out of his experience. That is, he wishes to extend and confirm his experience. The interest of his readers will be the same as his own, to extend and confirm their experience. Prejudice may prevent their doing so; new facts may modify old, new arguments engender new convictions. But the new knowledge and the fresh judgment must be assimilable to experience, or they will be rejected.

If the interpretation of history, then, is in terms of experience, it follows that the historical judgment of a man or group will conform to the historical experience of that man or group. Men's interest in history would indeed be narcissistic, were it not that what they perceive in history is not an image but a portrait.

[1]Jacques Barzun, "History, Popular and Unpopular" in *The Interpretation of History*, ed. by Joseph R. Strayer (Princeton, 1943), 50.
[2]R. G. Collingwood, *An Autobiography* (London, 1939), 37.

Reprinted from *University of Toronto Quarterly*, XV (3), April, 1946

It is for this reason that history is peculiarly the consolation of the conquered. To the oppressed the memory of past freedom gives hope in present despair; to the humiliated the recollection of past glory restores some measure of self-respect. It inspires, above all, the determination to survive. The independence of Eire, the nationalism of India, the survival of French Canada, point the observation.

History, so operating, is of course the history of folk-memory, of tale and ballad, or the work of the antiquarian and the genealogist, naive, mythic, usually tendentious, often inaccurate. Yet even "objective" history, the history of the academic scholar, works creatively in the social order whether by reinforcing tradition or by opening new paths of thought. However it may operate, it does operate—*e pur si muove*. Even though a given historical work were objective beyond the dictum of Becker (that every historian is biased at least in his determination not to be biased), it cannot fail to be part of the development of thought in its time, springing from it, pushing it forward, turning it into new channels.

The present argument is not meant, of course, as a condonation of partisanship in historical study. Rather it is a comment on that relativity of historical study in fields of limited reference, such as the nation, which Toynbee discusses in *A Study of History*. "In any age of any society," he remarks, "the study of history, like other social activities, is governed by the dominant tendencies of the time and place," and prefaces his discussion with a quotation from Xenophanes: "The Aethiopians say that their Gods are snub-nosed and black-skinned, and the Thracians that theirs are blue-eyed and red-haired. If only oxen and horses had hands and wanted to draw with their hands or to make the works of art that men make, then horses would draw the figures of their Gods like horses, and oxen like oxen, and would make their bodies on the models of their own."[3] The historian is part of the society he studies; it is only by increasing his frame of reference that he may diminish the relativity of his thought. Happy is he who escapes the perils of social anthropomorphism; the historian of colonial nationalism is the least likely to do so.

On Canadian history the foregoing remarks have a special bearing. Formed of the sherds of two empires, of fragments of Europe's most obstinate nationalities, cast down on the northern margin of habitable North America, the Canadian peoples were brought together in Confederation, not for the increase of liberty or the ends of justice, which were taken for granted, but to meet certain commercial, strategic, and imperial purposes. On the ancient imperial controls, dissolving under the acid of self-government, were imposed the new controls of federalism. The old imperialism was perpetuated in Sections 90 and 91 of the British North America Act of 1867. Before the old restraints had been forgotten, before communal and local rancours had been dissipated, there were new bonds to chafe at, a

[3]A. J. Toynbee, *A Study of History* (London, 1934), I, 1.

new claim to allegiance to stifle the simple loyalties of religion, race, and region.

Though the rights of Quebec were re-affirmed at Confederation, Quebec was faced with the prospect of an Ontario strengthened by a Protestant and Anglo-Saxon West, and the submergence of the French dispersion in a British sea. To whom the West? Nor was the West, except for British Columbia, to be admitted as an equal when population warranted: it was annexed as a subordinate territory, except for the grudging acknowledgment, in the creation of Manitoba, of Riel's resistance.

Thus there emerged the three decisive fields of Canadian historical interpretation: the French survival, the dominance of Ontario, and the subordination of the West, decisive in the sense that each is "an intelligible field of study" and in that each has its peculiar problems to be worked out in terms decisive for any interpretation of Canadian history as a whole. For the purpose of this essay, the maritime sections of Canada, both Atlantic and Pacific, may be set aside from consideration, not because they do not constitute fields of historical study of great interest and importance, or have not felt the Laurentian dominance, but because, susceptible as they are to the pull of their counterparts to the south and of imperial ties nourished by a common interest in the sea, they have always possessed destinies alternative to that of incorporation in Canada. Without them Canada in some sense might have been; without any one of the three "decisive" sections there could have been, in the larger sense of the name, no Canada.

It is in these three fields that the understanding of Canadian history as a whole is to be sought and found. What, then, has been the development of our historical knowledge of Canada so far?

In French Canada the theme from Garneau to Groulx has been survival, *la survivance canadienne-française.* That the faith, the language, and the civil law should continue has been the first imperative; the second is that the French be self-governing and equal to the English in Confederation. In British Canada, too, the emphasis has been on survival, for as the French were threatened by assimilation to the English, so the English were threatened by absorption into the United States. There was, too, the demand for self-government which triumphed as it cleared itself of the charge of being a prelude to annexation. This latter theme has been worked extensively by English-Canadian historians and has reached its climax in the work of Professors Kennedy and Martin.

Survival and self-government, that is, were the original themes of Canadian historical study. But these were narrowly political, essentially colonial, and were not infrequently developed in a somewhat antiquarian spirit. It is not surprising, therefore, that in recent years they should have been supplanted in English Canada by what may be termed the Laurentian theme: the metropolitan destiny of the St. Lawrence River, in pythonic struggle with the Hudson, to exploit economically and unite politically the northern half of the continent.

This new theme it is which flails new grain from the old straw of political history, which gives a certain unity to the history of the scattered pockets of settlement which are Canada, and reveals the drives of self-government and national consolidation. Irrigated by these waters the desert of Canadian history has produced at least two pages where only one fluttered before. Professor D. G. Creighton's *The Commercial Empire of the St. Lawrence* and *Dominion of the North*, with the allied work of Professors Innis and Lower on the staple trades, have raised Canadian history to major stature and given it a depth of meaning and brilliance of treatment comparable to any contemporary work.

Yet, handled though it is at the highest level of scholarship, this theme drives home one point, makes one ineffaceable impression: not by explicit statement, but in strong overtone it affirms the Laurentian dominance. For the historian cannot be neutral: he must judge deliberately or in default.

Thus it is of the greatest significance that when one turns to American history for a theme of comparable fructifying effect, one finds it in Turner's frontier thesis. In the frontier Turner found the American quality of American history. It was, according to this thesis, in virtue of the frontier experience that the American people became American. But, according to the Laurentian thesis, it was the commercial system of the St. Lawrence which made Canada, not a folk movement wringing from the harsh, common life of the frontier a national character and way of life, but a scheme of commercial exploitation, Hamiltonian in its politics, imperialistic in its methods, aiming not at political justice but at commercial profits.

It is, therefore, of the first importance to examine what the implications of the Laurentian thesis are for the future of historical studies in Canada, and for the national character they will help to shape.

In the first place, the Laurentian thesis is preoccupied with economic factors in the national history. This analysis of Canadian economic history begun by Adam Shortt almost two generations ago, was a very necessary part of the study of national development. The result was to reveal the preponderant part commercial monopoly and centralized business have played in that development from the great fur-trading companies to the vast concentrations of today. The total picture is that of a metropolitan economy, centering in Montreal and Toronto.

This is no doubt a correct representation of the actual facts. But economic thought is in its very nature deterministic. The divorce of economics and ethics was long since made absolute, and outside the moral sphere there is no freedom. That is, the Laurentian thesis is properly concerned with the play of economic factors, which follow the fleeting but irresistible lure of the price indices, and it has taken for granted what was irrelevant to it, namely, justice as between race and race and section and section.

Such an economically determined metropolitanism implies political imperialism, at least when the metropolitan power has competitors of equal or greater power. Pressed by American and British rivals, Canadian business could not enjoy the cheap profits of "informal" empire, to borrow C. R. Fay's phrase, as Britain could in the nineteenth and the United States can in the twentieth century. Confederation was brought about to realize the commercial potentialities of the St. Lawrence. Where self-government existed it was recognized; where the people of territory annexed resisted, it was granted but starved of the means to live; where they had an alternative and were too distant to be intimidated, it was granted in full. But there was nothing like the American Ordinance of 1787, providing for the automatic extension of freedom with population, every sixty thousandth free inhabitant bringing statehood with him,[4] no colonial policy making the extension of Canadian rule concomitant with the spread of self-government; there was only from 1869 to 1930 the old hateful wrangle by which Eastern Canada had formerly worried Downing Street into granting responsible government. An interpretation of history in economic terms, of necessity follows the pattern of commercial imperialism it undertakes to trace.

From commercial monopoly and political centralization to cultural uniformity the step is short. When a commercial empire has been founded and a federal union set up, it is almost impossible in the twentieth century not to assume that a nation too has been created, or is in process of creation. But there are in fact two nationalities and four geographical sections in the Canadian union.

The implications of the Laurentian thesis are, then, a metropolitan economy, a political imperialism of the metropolitan area, and uniformity of the metropolitan culture throughout the hinterlands. It is not asserted that any of the scholars who have developed this theme have stated these implications categorically, or necessarily intended them. They are submitted as a fair deduction from the thesis as expounded. No quarrel, of course, is intended with the thesis as such. To repeat, it is a legitimate approach to Canadian history; its results are the most enlightening yet achieved in Canadian historical scholarship. Among scholars and intelligent laymen it can have none but stimulating and fruitful effects.

But the danger inherent in it will become apparent when, after many processes of digestion at least as crude as that to which it has been subjected here, the Laurentian thesis percolates downward into the text-book and the schoolroom. Then its implications cannot but be misleading both to those brought up in the metropolitan area and those brought up in the hinterlands. Teaching inspired by the historical experience of metropolitan Canada cannot but deceive, and deceive cruelly, children of the outlying sections. Their experience after school will contradict the instruction of the history class, and develop in them that dichotomy which characterizes

[4]The Ordinance, of course, provided for retention of control of public lands by the federal government, as did the Manitoba Act of 1870 (Section 30).

all hinterland Canadians, a nationalism cut athwart by a sense of sectional injustice.

For Confederation was brought about to increase the wealth of Central Canada, and until that original purpose is altered, and the concentration of wealth and population by national policy in Central Canada ceases, Confederation must remain an instrument of injustice.

As long as the sense of sectional injustice remains, and as long as the French feel that they are not admitted to equality in Confederation, there can be no commonly acceptable interpretation of Canadian history and no common text-book, as proposed two years ago, for Canadian schools. For the interpretation of Canadian history which will satisfy the experience of British Canada will contradict that of French Canada; and so for Central Canada and the West.

For indeed the sectionalism of the West is, in different terms, as justified as the French nationalism of Quebec or the British nationalism of Ontario. Turner's comparison of the sections of the American union to the nations of Europe is relevant to Canada also. Not only is there driven between East and West the blunt wedge of the Shield. Not only is there the clash of economic interest caused by difference in resources, climate, and stage of economic development. There are also environmental differences so great as to be seldom appreciated. The West is plains country, with few, though great resources, a harsh and hazardous climate, and an inflexible economy. So domineering is this environment that it must change people and institutions greatly from those of the humid forest regions of the East. The West, for example, has long faced the problem of paying fixed rates of interest with returns from a very "unfixed" rainfall.

There is finally the fact that the West was annexed to Confederation as a subordinate region and so remained for sixty years. Such was the historical schooling of the West. It had, therefore, to fight its way up to self-government and equality in Confederation, nor is the process ended. No more than French Canada can the West accept a common interpretation of Canadian history or a cultural metropolitanism. The West must first work out its own historical experience (a task well begun by Professor A. S. Morton and Major G. F. Stanley), and free itself, and find itself. Until it ceases to be either an exploited or a subsidized region it cannot do so. In an imperfect world an unequal incidence of national policies is no doubt inevitable, but even in an imperfect world people may be allowed to shape an interpretation of history and a way of life in accord with their own experience.

If this view appears extreme, it is partly because Westerners seldom enjoy that blessed moderation which descends on those who have dwelt long among the flesh-pots, and partly because metropolitan Canada has seldom appreciated the impact of Laurentian imperialism on the West. One's appreciation of a club depends entirely upon the end from which one contemplates it. It was the fate of the West to become the colony of a colony which brought to its new imperial role neither imagination, liberality, nor magnanimity. To ensure returns from the £300,000 spent in "buying" the West, the natural resources were retained, contrary to British precedent, the protective tariff, that chief of Canadian extractive industries, was established, and the monopoly clause of the Canadian Pacific Railway charter was imposed. In the events which preceded the rebellion of 1885, Ottawa added neglect to subordination, and after the rebellion was suppressed, neglect from time to time was not unknown.

And Eastern aggression has continued in other and sometimes subtler ways. For two generations the West has been led by the Ontario-born. What this has meant it would be idle to attempt to estimate, but it may be that native Westerners will not be so susceptible to the blandishments of metropolitan "nationalism." On the other hand, the Westerner, like the medieval Scot, is poor. Similar in effect is the fact that the West, like a colony, is used as a proving ground in which bright young men in business and the professions prepare themselves for higher positions in the head offices of the East. How familiar, and how touching, is the figure of the Ontario professor awaiting, in Ovidian exile, the call that will take him back to Toronto!

> Si quis adhuc istic meminit Nasonis adempti,
> et superest sine me nomen in urbe meum,
> suppositum stellis numquam tangentibus aequor
> me sciat in media vivere barbaria.[5]

Such dominance, however, higher civilizations, be it said without irony, always assert over lower.

Be that as it may, the subordination of the West, when added to its sharp sectionalism, gives it an incisive and cogent character of its own. This it is which makes it the third of the "decisive" areas of Canadian historical study. It has no acceptable alternative to working out its own identity in terms of its own historical experience. It must realize its latent nationalism, a nationalism neither racial like the French nor dominant—a "garrison" nationality—like that of Ontario, but environmental and, because of the diversity of its people, composite. It may, of course, fail (as the French might have been assimilated), and, by the joint process of exploitation and loss of its natural leaders to the East and the United States, be reduced to a subject people, without character or spirit.

Yet if it takes up the old Canadian struggle for survival and self-government, it may survive and, with French Canada, end the Laurentian domination. When all of the "decisive" and subordinate areas have achieved survival and self-government, and have raised themselves to equality in Confederation, when Confederation is held together no longer by the "Protestant garrison" and protectionist imperialism, but by the consent of equals, when it ceases to be an instrument of domination and exploitation and becomes a means to co-operation and distributive justice,

[5]*Tristia*, III, x, 1-4.

then there can be a common interpretation of Canadian history and a common text-book in the schools, French as well as English, West as well as East. Moreover, it must be a catholic, imaginative, and magnanimous interpretation. This is not only ideally desirable, it is practically necessary. The Canadian state cannot be devoted to absolute nationalism, the focus of a homogeneous popular will. The two nationalities and the four sections of Canada forbid it. The state in Canada must promote liberty of persons and communities, and justice, which is the essence of liberty. Canadians may well note Acton's words:

No power can so efficiently resist the tendencies of centralization, of corruption, and of absolutism, as that community which is the vastest that can be included in a State, which imposes on its members a consistent similarity of character, interest, and opinion, and which arrests the action of the sovereign by the influence of a divided patriotism. The presence of different nations under the same sovereignty is similar in its effect to the independence of the Church in the State. It provides against servility, which flourishes under the shadow of a single authority, by balancing interests, multiplying associations, and giving to the subject the restraint and support of combined opinion. In the same way it promotes independence by forming definite groups of public opinion, and by affording a great source and centre of political sentiments, and of notions of duty not derived from the sovereign will. Liberty provokes diversity, and diversity preserves liberty by supplying the means of organization. . . . The co-existence of several nations under the same State is a test, as well as the best security of its freedom. It is also one of the chief instruments of civilization, and, as such, belongs to the natural and providential order, and indicates a state of greater advancement than the national unity which is the ideal of modern liberalism.[6]

That might almost have been composed as the ideal of Canadian national development; it is certainly the only practicable course for the future. Until it is accepted as such generally, by both nationalities and all sections, it is premature to suggest a common text-book in history or to propose to add cultural to economic metropolitanism.

[6]Lord Acton, *The History of Freedom and Other Essays* (London, 1907), 289-90.

Sir John Macdonald and Canadian Historians

D. G. CREIGHTON

I

JOHN ALEXANDER MACDONALD was born on January 11, 1815, and died on June 6, 1891. Of the seventy-six years of his long life, well over half—forty-seven in all—were passed amid the agitations of Canadian politics. He was elected to parliament in 1844, when he was not yet thirty; he became a minister of the Crown in 1847, when he had just turned thirty-two. For over ten years under the system of the dual premiership which obtained in the old Province of Canada, he was one of the two principal leaders of government; and for nineteen years he was prime minister of the new Dominion. It is an astonishing record— astonishing, and, as a whole, unique. It is true that Mr. Mackenzie King has been prime minister of the Dominion of Canada for a longer period than Sir John Macdonald. But Macdonald's career of leadership stretches back beyond Confederation; and his record as a whole, in both the Province and the Dominion, is unsurpassed and probably unsurpassable.

The very length and variety of a career which spanned so much of Canada's history and touched so many of its activities pose a question which is, perhaps, of general interest to Canadian historians. What have we done with the man who lived for nearly fifty years at the centre of Canada's political affairs and who dominated them for over twenty-five? What have we done with the five hundred volumes of his papers which lie in the Archives at Ottawa, with the monumental mass of government documents, parliamentary debates, newspapers, periodicals, pamphlets, memoirs, and autobiographies which record his multifarious activities in neutral, complimentary, or abusive terms? It seems a fair question to ask—a reasonable test to apply to Canadian historiography. How do Canadian historians measure up to it? It may

Reprinted from *Canadian Historical Review*, XXIX (1), March, 1948 be that, in an effort to answer this question, we shall come upon certain qualities, or characteristic features, of Canadian historical writing which are worthy of critical reflection.

There are, to begin with, two curious and unexpected facts to be noticed about the biographical literature on Macdonald. In the first place, there is not very much of it; and in the second place, what there is is not new, but relatively old. In the years immediately preceding and following Macdonald's death, when his career was at its end and his reputation at its apogee, there appeared several biographies of him, written with little concern for form, and in a spirit of uncritical laudation, of which the best, by long odds, because at least it was based upon the documents, was Sir Joseph Pope's two-volume study. These were followed, after a long interval, by Sir George Parkin's volume in the original "Makers of Canada" series; and this in turn, after a further and longer interval, by Mr. W. S. Wallace's short biographical sketch. There the procession ended. It ended, curiously and incomprehensibly, in the middle nineteen-twenties, at the very moment when historical scholarship in Canada was already launched upon a sustained and comprehensive attack on the problems of Canadian history. And it has not been resumed. The thirty years from 1918 to 1948 have witnessed a minor revolution in the study of Canadian history; but they have added very little to the biographical literature on Sir John Macdonald.

This is not to say, of course, that the work of these years has contributed nothing to our knowledge of Macdonald's career, or to our understanding of his personality. Within limits, it has done both. During the last twenty years the Macdonald Papers in Ottawa have been raided by a small company of scholars for all sorts of purposes, and in pursuit of all kinds of themes—national and regional, political, constitutional, military, and economic. But the interest of these scholars in Macdonald has been secondary, not primary, and sometimes even accidental. They have, so to speak, walked all round Macdonald without troubling to look at him. They have taken him for granted, mainly because they were preoccupied with other matters, partly because they assumed that they knew all about him anyway. Almost nothing has been done to examine, correct, or justify the traditional picture of Macdonald—the picture, half legend and folk-lore, of the easy-going, pleasure-loving, and none too scrupulous opportunist, who survived a half-century of political conflict by means of a dubious series of compromises, appeasements, and reconciliations.

Now there may be a single, simple, and sufficient explanation for these calm assumptions and this evident neglect. Canadian history, even when it is regarded as a part of the history of either the British Empire or the North American continent, is possibly a parochial, not to say limited, theme. It attracts a few enthusiastic scholars; but their number will never be very large; and, though their work has acquired a certain popularity at the present moment, both publishers and public have not shown a great deal of interest in it in the past, and may possibly show as little in the future. All this may be enough, and more than enough, to account for the slow and uneven progress of Canadian historical research, for the unaccountable gaps and lamentable omissions in Canadian historical literature. Possibly. And yet the explanation seems somehow unsatisfactory. It explains too much or too little. It has little light to throw upon the direction and the character of the work which has actually been produced. Perhaps it is worthwhile to pursue the matter a little further, to approach a little more closely the problem of Canadian history and Canadian historical biography in general, and of the biography of Macdonald in particular.

II

Biography is a distinct and special branch of historical writing. Of all branches it is perhaps most closely related to the art of the novel, and this in both a legitimate and an illegitimate sense. In a biography, as in a novel, the phases of historical development, the conflict of historical forces, are seen, not in generalities and abstractions, but concretely, in terms of a central, main character, a set of subordinate characters, and a series of particular situations. A biography may achieve the vividness and actuality of a novel; but, with even greater ease and frequency, it may degenerate into the trivial, or dull, improbability of fiction and propaganda. The complex facts may be cheerfully disregarded for the sake of dramatic simplicity, or they may be deliberately perverted for the purpose of political justification. And all too frequently, therefore, historical characters come to be divided into two broad classes; those who look like appropriate figures for melodrama, and those who appear to be required subjects for political panegyric. On the one hand, there is the light-hearted, fictional biography with its gaudy jacket which has been written with a keen eye, not so much for facts, as for sales; and on the other, there is the solemn work of commemoration, usually in two fat funereal volumes, which looks, as Lytton Strachey observed, as if it had been composed by the undertaker, as the final item of his job. These are the two extremes of historical biography in English; and in the late nineteenth and twentieth centuries fashionable practice has tended to alternate between them in certain fairly well-marked cycles or periods.

Canada has never passed through these alternating phases. It would have been better if it had. But in this, as in so many other aspects of our literary development, our experience has been almost entirely vicarious. It may be, of course, that we have derived some indirect profit from the more daring experiments of others. We may perhaps no longer act the part of historical undertakers in quite the same obvious way as when Alexander Mackenzie wrote his life of George Brown, or Joseph Pope composed his biography of Sir John Macdonald. But we still seem to lack, what the fictional biography might at least have taught us, a lively interest in character and personality. Canadian biographies have a formal, official air, as if they had been written out of the materials of a newspaper morgue, or from the resources of a library largely composed of Blue Books and Sessional Papers. In all too many cases, the subject remains an important Public Personage—in capitals—dwarfed by the circumstances of his "Times," which are portrayed in great chunks of descriptive material, pitilessly detailed, and among which he drags out an embarrassed and attenuated documentary existence, like an unsubstantial *papier maché* figure made up of old dispatches and newspaper files. It seems difficult for us even to make our characters recognizably different; and as one reads through a small shelf-full of Canadian biographies, one is aware of a growing and uncomfortable sensation that one is reading about one and the same man. Is it possible that, even in Canada, people can actually be so indistinguishably alike? Is there really only one Canadian statesman, whose metamorphoses have merely involved a change of name? Or are all Canadian statesmen simply members of the same family, a spiritual family at any rate, with certain persistent and unchangeable family characteristics, and a distinguished hyphenated surname? Are there really biographies of Baldwin, Hincks, and Laurier, or are these merely lives of Robert Responsible-Government and Francis Responsible-Government, and Wilfrid Responsible-Government?

Now this abstract and inhuman method of presentation, which may be called the Procedure Appropriate for the Portrayal of

Public Personages, is damaging enough to most historical characters, but completely fatal to Macdonald. It is a nineteenth and
twentieth-century historical technique; and Macdonald, though
his entire political career lies within the reign of Queen Victoria,
was never an exemplary and typical Victorian statesman. In
some important ways at least, his affinities seem to lie rather with
the eighteenth and early nineteenth century than with his own
age; and, at any rate, the materials which he left behind him are
not, in many cases, easily susceptible of manipulation by the
methods of the standard biography. He could, and did, make
some great speeches; but both in the earliest and the latest periods
of his career he was often a casual and indifferent speaker. The
great state papers of his career were often written by others,
notably by A. T. Galt; and, even more important, some of his
most characteristic habits of thought and methods of action are
traceable, if at all, through the stray hints and oblique references
of his private letters, or of other still more scattered and fugitive
evidence. It is difficult to make a standard biography of his life;
Pope's effort proved that; and, therefore, perhaps the first reason
for the failure to grapple efficiently with Macdonald's career lies
in a certain immaturity of craftsmanship, which is as much
literary as historical.

III

A second reason is to be found surely in the strong partisan
tone of a good deal of Canadian historical writing. Macdonald
was a Conservative; and throughout Canadian historiography
there is easily discernible a stiff strain of Liberalism with a
capital L. It would not be very difficult, and it might be amusing,
to compile a list of Canadian historians and political scientists
who have been editors of Liberal newspapers, cabinet ministers in
Liberal administrations, deputy ministers, heads of boards, and
members of Royal Commissions appointed by Liberal Govern-
ments. In respect of the latter of these gentlemen, it is not
necessarily implied that appointment, in their case, was a kind of
public recognition of strict party fidelity; but, in the state in
which Canadian politics were and perhaps still are, the evidence
is, to say the least, suggestive. The list would not be a very short
one; and it might be supplemented by a further list of historians
and political scientists who have, so to speak, shared the Liberal
ethic and contributed to the growth of the Liberal interpretation
of Canadian history.

This interpretation has, in the first place, its solemn side, its aspect heroic and almost sacred, with prophets like Baldwin, wise kings like Lord Elgin, great moments of deliverance from bondage as with the formation of the Reform Ministry in 1848 and terrible plagues and tribulations as when Metcalfe and Head were sent to smite the chosen people. It has also its familiar and popular side; and it is to be hoped that what might be called the Liberal folk-lore of Canadian history will some day be investigated scientifically, as has already been done with the rhymes of Mother Goose. But these sagas and fairy tales are not the whole of the Grit interpretation of Canadian history; much of it is straightforward, hard-hitting journalism. There are moments when almost any book on Canadian affairs during the nineteenth century begins to sound like a string of *Globe* editorials; there are times when every treatise on external relations during the twentieth century begins to echo the confident ring of the leaders in the *Winnipeg Free Press*. The tone is unmistakably journalistic; and yet, curiously enough, it is perhaps the journalists—and particularly J. S. Willison—who have kept the greatest measure of detachment. And there are few more diverting passages in Canadian historical writing than the paragraphs in which the journalists, Willison and Dafoe, rebuke the insinuations and correct the errors of that eminent scholar, Dr. Oscar Douglas Skelton, Ph.D.

Every historian must have a point-of-view; but it will be valuable to his readers precisely to the extent to which it escapes from the parochial and transitory. If it is based upon some general view of man and society, if it is built up in accordance with the rules of independent craftsmanship, if it is shaped by a strict theory of art, then it may be an inextinguishable source of illumination and delight. Gibbon took his stand upon the broad, substantial ground of the eighteenth century, upon its values— moral, intellectual, and artistic—of scepticism and urbanity, of moderation and harmony, of symmetry and balance. Macaulay's point-of-vantage was at once more exiguous and more impermanent. He was a complacent child of early nineteenth-century Whig politics and the early nineteenth-century Industrial Revolution. He was a Philistine, a materialist, a bigoted partisan, with an over-emphatic, debating style. As a political and social philosopher, he was damned; but what saved him was his high conception of the historian's vocation and his unflagging devotion to the art of narrative prose.

Canadian historians, in all too many cases, commit Macaulay's mistakes, without the excuse of his virtues. Rarely does one feel that they have taken their stand upon a broad, general philosophy and within the frame-work of a great literary tradition. They are apt to be parochial, contemporary, and argumentative. Even the ramparts of modern scholarship do not seem to have made it a great deal easier for them to maintain their critical judgment or their independence of spirit. Their values often seem to have a disturbingly close approximation to the planks of one of the party platforms of their period of study. And to view Canadian history through mass-produced spectacles such as these is simply a bore. Canadian affairs in the nineteenth century, like English affairs in the seventeenth and eighteenth, are interesting because they concern human beings confronted with human situations and human problems of permanent and universal importance. But to watch this varied and changing spectacle from one side or other of the House of Commons at Ottawa, with somebody nudging you in the ribs every second moment, is to undergo an experience of colossal tedium.

This tradition of partisanship in its narrowest sense may derive, in part, from the relative unimportance of universities in Canada during the nineteenth century, and from the dominance of journalism and politics in Canada's intellectual life. Nobody in the nineteenth century seemed to be able to do much to check this prevailing tendency; and one man who might have flung the whole weight of his considerable influence against it, failed miserably and completely to do so. This was Goldwin Smith. Smith, who had been professor of history at Oxford, enjoyed a high prestige at the moment when he arrived in Canada in the early eighteen-seventies. He possessed a genuinely lively mind, a wide range of knowledge, a rich experience of men and affairs, and a fluent and pointed style. In that atmosphere of agitated and unreasoning prejudice which was Canada in the eighteen-seventies and eighties, he might have stood up for the values of detachment, urbanity, and moderation. He might, if he willed, have represented civilization. A following was waiting for him, for a group of young men, the members of the so-called Canada First party, were honestly sick of the malevolence, abuse, and corruption of the politics of the time. But he failed them. It is not too much to say that he disappointed an entire generation of Canadians.

It is true, of course, that he posed as what he might have been, but never was. He kept on signing his little articles with the pseudonym "A Bystander"; and, oddly enough, it is this conception of him which has imposed itself upon posterity. In reality, nobody was ever less of a bystander than he. He was an intellectual partisan, a coldly furious intellectual partisan, but a partisan all the same, like everybody else. He was a journalist among other journalists, a propagandist among other propagandists, and not very different from his fellows in either category, except that he had a sharper pen and a longer purse than most. It is true that he quarrelled with both the old parties in turn, and it is possible that his personality was one of the main factors in the disintegration of Canada First. But these successive estrangements by no means implied an attitude of serene and Olympian detachment. They simply meant that Goldwin Smith was a one-man party, that he was the Goldwin Smith party, to which he attached himself with all his petulant vanity and rancorous vindictiveness. Indeed, if he is to be distinguished from his fellows at all, it will probably be not by the deficiency, but by the excess of his partisanship. Beneath his restrained and slightly donnish exterior, there seethed and bubbled the most extraordinary mixture of venomous resentments and hatreds. Almost invariably —at least when he wrote of Canadian affairs—he was a debater, a debater who composed mainly for definite political occasions and for particular political purposes, a debater who always fought to win. The points of his arguments, like small, flat-headed nails bought by the keg from the parliamentary debating ironmongery, are invariably nailed in with the greatest precision and agility; and the thoughts themselves are often as thin and flat and brittle, as unvarying and invariable as shingles. Always in reading him, one is conscious of the uneasy impression that some large and important consideration has been conveyed away, surreptitiously and with the greatest possible lack ' of ostentation, under the apparently comfortable assumption that its absence will never be noticed. It is like describing Niagara with the Horseshoe Falls left out, or painting a picture of the Toronto sky-line minus the Royal York Hotel.

This ingrained disposition to partisanship has been weakened with time; this hard debating style has been dulled by academic caution, possibly to the disadvantage of Canadian prose style. But the old tradition lasted well into the twentieth century and its effects are not yet entirely dissipated. It would be too much to say that there are no modern biographies of Macdonald because there are too many Grit historians; but there is a small kernel of truth in the remark, and it may stand. The obvious misrepresentation of actions, the easy imputation of unworthy motives, the facile condemnation based on scarcely concealed political preferences—these transparent manoeuvres we have learnt largely, if not entirely, to avoid. But back of these particular biases lay a far more general and fundamental prepossession—a prepossession which, if it did not impel us to misrepresent, at least prevented us from understanding. We had ceased, or were ceasing, to be converts to party programmes; but we had fallen victims to the nationalist interpretation of Canadian history.

IV

The chief characteristic of nationalist history has been a preoccupation, amounting almost to an obsession, with the twin achievements of Responsible Government and Dominion Status. And it is through this obsession that the concept of Canadian nationality has been largely shaped. The development of Canada's national autonomy has been identified almost exclusively with the process of emancipation from British control, and the process of emancipation itself has been represented, all too often, as a continuous struggle between legitimate colonial demand and obscurantist imperial resistance. These interpretations have both narrowed and distorted our understanding of Canadian national growth; they have virtually eliminated one main theme in the history of that development and they have left the other misshapen and unconvincing. For obviously the reality of Canadian nationality depends as much upon the separateness of Canada in North America as upon its autonomy within the British Empire; and obviously also the winning of autonomy within the Empire has not been a continuous hateful struggle, but a long process of bargaining, adjustment, and reorganization, in which, not infrequently, the initiative came from the Mother Country rather than from the colony. Nationalist history has, on the whole, shown astonishingly little interest in either of these evident facts. The achievement and maintenance of Canadian separateness in the North American continent have either been neglected or have been represented, in the main, as an easy and perfunctory business, in sharp contrast with the unending and acrimonious conflict by which automony within the British Empire has been achieved. Inevitably, therefore, "imperialism" was identified simply and exclusively with British imperialism. Other "imperialisms" were suppositious, and fictitious: British imperialism alone was horribly real.

There can be little doubt that these assumptions were central in the body of popular nationalist thought which was urged so vociferously by politicians and publicists in the period before the War of 1939-45. It is to be hoped that, in the near future, the nationalism of that era will be subjected to a curious and careful scrutiny, for it is an attractive subject, with lots of easily available evidence, since the nationalists spread themselves so copiously and vehemently upon the record. Obviously this analysis cannot be begun here; but it may at least be said that two of the frequent, normal, and almost inevitable ingredients of pre-war nationalism were a lively dislike of Great Britain and the British Empire and a respectful admiration for the institutions and forms of life of the United States. Indeed it might be suggested that, in certain cases at least, nationalist feeling was not primary at all, but secondary and derivative—that it was, in fact, a function which depended for its value upon two other factors, and was almost invariably expressed in terms of them.

Whatever the ultimate source of their impulses, the nationalists set out, with a fair degree of unanimity, to rescue Canada from the discredit of its all too British past and to rehabilitate it as a decent American community. J. W. Dafoe's *Canada: An American Nation* (the omission of the word "North" is not entirely without significance) is an example of this kind of effort, on a high level; and there were other and lower levels which were successfully reached and plumbed by the books and articles of the period. It began to be popular to portray the English Canadian as a typical North American, virtually indistinguishable from his neighbour to the South, a little stolid perhaps, a little slow—slowness was, indeed, one of his few admitted distinctive characteristics, and it was generally agreed that he was about a quarter century behind the Times—but plodding bravely onward in his great neighbour's wake and determined to realize his personality in his great neighbour's image. It was true, to be sure, that his political institutions were regrettably monarchical; but from the time of the King-Byng controversy, there was an evident inclination, which became at times a determined effort, to republicanize these institutions in the popular imagination. In the autumn of 1945, when Mr. Ilsley attempted to define the constitutional position of the cabinet to the House of Commons, the resulting general discussion afforded some curious evidence as to just how far this process had gone. Mr. Ilsley's constitutionally correct statement that "the authority of government is received from the Crown" evoked strong criticism, not only from the opposition parties in parliament, but also from certain Liberal newspapers in the country. This criticism was apparently based upon the assumption that there was some fundamental conflict between the principle that the authority of government is derived from the Crown, and the principle that government is responsible to the House of Commons and the electorate; and this, in turn, may very well have had its origin in the more fundamental, if inarticulate, premise that government could not be "democratic" unless it was republican. We have travelled a long distance since 1867. In that year, the Fathers of Confederation struggled to obtain the title "Kingdom of Canada"; and in the decade before the War of 1914-18, this was still the ultimate objective of a man like J. S. Ewart. But nowadays, though many people at Ottawa are obviously tired of the word "Dominion," nobody apparently would dream of applying the word "Kingdom" to a country which is in fact a monarchy.

For historians, the most interesting feature of this whole movement is the effect which it may have had upon Canadian history. Already, of course, Canadian history was reasonably well adjusted to the new nationalist temper. The main staple of that history was the chronicle of the valiant and persistent efforts by which British North America had extracted Responsible Government and Dominion Status from a grudging and resisting Great Britain. This was much; but, in the new frame of mind, it was clearly not enough. Themes more eloquently expressive of Canada's destiny in the New World were required. If the country was to have a typical North American future, then surely it must have had a typical North American past. A normal American community, virtually indistinguishable from the United States, it must have been moved by the same impulses and governed by the same forces as the American republic; and the two countries must have passed through similar tribulations and comparable stages of development. This chain of reasoning may not have been so logically worked out by Canadian historians; they may have been moved merely by a desire to broaden the scope of their research. But, in any case, there can be little doubt as to the new direction which was given to Canadian history. Scholars began to import large chunks of American history into their Canadian historical studies, making comparisons, pointing out resemblances, drawing analogies, and using terminology and concepts derived from American history with the greatest gusto and abandon.

One of the early manifestations of this new movement in Canadian historical thought was the publication in 1927 of W. B. Munro's Marfleet Lectures given at the University of Toronto on *American Influences on Canadian Government*. It became fashionable, in the years that followed, to insist that Canadian politics was a British game played according to American rules, or an American game played according to British rules (I am afraid I have forgotten the exact form the epigram took); but evidently its clear implication was that though the form of the game might be British, its vital reality was American—American in the sense in which the word is used by citizens of the United States. Ideas such as these meant obviously a strong bias towards environmentalism; and environmental notions were still more clearly indicated in the amazingly ubiquitous use of the concept of the frontier. For a time the frontier was dragged in at every opportunity, appropriate or otherwise. It was used to explain almost anything, particularly anything that was new, dynamic, and vaguely forward-looking. It explained Mackenzie, the rebellion, the Clear Grit movement; there were even times when it seemed that it was going to explain the entire course of Canadian Liberalism. As for the Reformers and Liberals, they became practically the same as Jeffersonian and Jacksonian Democrats; while the Conservatives, on their part, were made to appear almost identical with Hamiltonian Federalists or with Republicans. Finally, and this was perhaps the most heroic effort of all, an attempt was occasionally made to prove that Canadian relations with the United States had been fairly amicable throughout, or, at any rate, that the main disagreement between the two countries had been exacerbated out of all recognition by the bunglings of British diplomacy.

It is not likely that we shall ever understand Macdonald or his times through the uncritical use of concepts and methods of this kind. The balance of our historical interpretation, which may have stood in need of rectification a quarter century ago, has now clearly fallen too far on the other side. The rather simple-minded environmentalism of the past twenty-five years stands in obvious need of a careful re-examination. We should ask ourselves what we mean by treating the North American environment as a solid, undifferentiated bloc; we should pay more attention to the cultural baggage, to the ideas and values, of the people who developed it; and, above all, we should begin to treat those ideas with some respect, without instantly rejecting about one-half of

them—usually the half that we do not happen to like—as fraudu-
lent and time-serving.   Sir John Macdonald lived, not in the
twentieth, but in the nineteenth century; and the English Canada
of his days was largely a provincial society, a section of a larger
British community, which was still, in many important ways, a
unity, culturally and spiritually, as well as in the realm of politics,
diplomacy, defence, and finance.   For Canadians the two capitals
of their world were Ottawa and London; these cities were almost
equally important to Macdonald and to those with whom he
worked.   He knew them both—lived in them both—in London,
on one occasion, for several months; and to the end of his days
the holiday that he enjoyed most was a trip to the capital of the
Empire.

Frontierism,
Metropolitanism, and Canadian History

J. M. S. CARELESS

LIKE any other history, that of Canada has been written within the framework of intellectual concepts, some of which have been consciously applied by historians, while others have shaped their work more or less indirectly through the influence of the surrounding climate of opinion. It would obviously be impossible to draw out and catalogue all the concepts that have affected the writing of Canadian history, even in the most general way. Yet it does seem possible to discern certain underlying ideas or patterns of thought that have given character to various phases of Canadian historiography. And in more recent times, in particular, one can note the powerful influence of what might be called (for want of a more precise term) "frontierism" in the history of Canada.

The idea of the dynamic frontier as a great and distinctive force moulding North American development has left an enduring mark on the writing of history in Canada, just as it has in the United States. No doubt this frontier idea is no longer as fresh and vital in its application to this country as it was in the period before the Second World War: indeed, it is largely because its original influence has declined, and the concept has thus become a historical phenomenon in itself, that we are entitled to discuss and assess its influence. Nor was the frontier thesis proper, as propounded by Frederick Jackson Turner and elaborated by his disciples, ever adopted as fully or dogmatically in Canada as it was in the United States—and there, of course, it has long been the subject of qualification and criticism. Nevertheless, the frontier interpretation broadly affected the thinking of a number of distinguished Canadian historians who in the main began their work about a quarter-century ago.[1] Today we can hardly examine the current state of Canadian historiography, and perhaps project its lines of growth, without giving heavy weight to the North American–environmentalist view of our history which stemmed originally from Turner's frontier thesis and which still leaves a rich heritage on both sides of the Canadian-American boundary.

[1]It is worthy of note that the *Canadian Historical Review* for September, 1932 (XII, no. 3, 343), in recording the death of F. J. Turner in March of that year, observed: "His emphasis on the importance of the frontier was the greatest single influence in the re-interpretation of the history of the United States during the past generation. The application of his views to Canadian history has scarcely begun but it is safe to say that they will have a profound effect—perhaps not less in emphasizing the differences than the similarities in the development of the two countries."

Reprinted from *Canadian Historical Review*, XXXV (1), March, 1954

There were other approaches to Canadian history before the rise of frontierism, and at present there are still others, which may involve the modification, complication, or even the virtual reversal of the frontier concept. Accordingly, in order to put frontierism in its proper context, it is first necessary to generalize—rather alarmingly, perhaps—on several "schools" of Canadian history. Each of these had some sort of interpretative approach, or at least some underlying assumptions, which gave a broadly similar character to the works its members produced.

These schools, however, are being set forth merely for convenience in tracing the general patterns of Canadian historiography and not as an all-inclusive filing system; for when individual historians are considered they do not always fit neatly into one particular classification. Some may change their school allegiance with the passage of time, while others, so to speak, may fall between schools. Furthermore, since the writing of history in French- and English-speaking Canada has largely been carried on as two separate enterprises, it would be of small consequence to try to link French-language schools with the English ones to be established below. And yet, despite these limitations, it can still be asserted that at various stages in Canadian historiography certain general approaches have been followed by important groups of historians, so that the designating of "schools" to illuminate that fact is by no means an unprofitable exercise.

I

The first school to be so designated might be termed the Britannic, or Blood is Thicker than Water School. The writers of this group were often convinced imperialists of the later nineteenth or early twentieth centuries and were closely attached in sentiment and background to Great Britain. They tended, as William Kingsford, that dull dean of Canadian historians, said he did, to make their theme the emergence of a new Britannic community within the empire, a part of one imperial organism, whose people enjoyed the British institutions of their forefathers and were worthy members of that indefinable company, the "British race."[2] This Britannic

[2]William Kingsford, *The History of Canada* (10 vols., Toronto, 1887–98). For his declaration of purpose, see particularly the prefaces to volumes VII, VIII, and X. Other historians who might be named to the Britannic school are Sir George Parkin, J. C. Dent, A. G. Bradley, Archibald MacMechan, and James Hannay. Of the works of the last-named, see especially *How Canada Was Held for the Empire: The Story of the War of 1812* (Toronto, 1905), a later edition of his *War of 1812* (1901), whose very title is significant.

School was inclined to ignore North American forces except when they were concentrated in the threatening power of the United States. The defeat of American pressure from without in 1776, 1812, and 1867 had "kept Canada British." So much for North America: a foe to be resisted.

Yet this group contributed something of lasting significance to the thought of Canadian history: the idea that Canada represented a declaration of independence from the United States, an attempt to build a second community in North America outside the American republic, and one marked off from it, indeed, by the longer persistence of the imperial tie. For some time this Canadian community would look to the bond with Britain to offset American dangers. But in the young twentieth century, when the days of actual threat had passed, that bond seemed to change increasingly in its implication—from protection to subordination. It was now that another school of Canadian historians began to arise, who viewed the imperial tie more critically in the light of the growing spirit of nationalism. And their main theme now became the march of Canada to political nationhood, through many a parliamentary manœuvre and struggle of words as colonial limitations were progressively overcome.

This new School of Political Nationhood chiefly concentrated on the paper-strewn path to national status, directing Canadian history to Colonial Office dispatches, the records of imperial conferences, and tense questions of treaty-making powers. Two phases, however, may be discerned in the writings of this school, though both were concerned with the peaceful and piecemeal evolution of Canada to nationhood. The first of these mainly treated the achievement of responsible government and confederation, and on the whole was favourably disposed to things British, since leading historians like Chester Martin and R. G. Trotter saw these national advances as being considerably aided by British advocacy and still as taking shape within the general framework of British institutions.[3] As this indicates, there was really no sharp break here

[3]See especially Chester Martin, *Empire and Commonwealth* (Oxford, 1929) and R. G. Trotter, *Canadian Federation* (Toronto, 1924). Others who might be considered members of this school are Adam Shortt, in his writings outside the specialized field of economic history, William Smith, G. E. Wilson, D. C. Harvey, Chester New, and perhaps G. M. Wrong. It will be seen, of course, that one school may overlap another in point of time, and draw its members from more than one generation. It bears repeating, however, that no attempt will or can be made to classify all major historians in one school or another. Some by virtue of fairly specialized subject-matter may defy a broad classification, despite the importance of their work. Scholars primarily concerned with the French régime, the federal system, or regional develop-

between the Britannic and Nationhood schools, and contemporary opinion in Canada largely tended to think in terms both of national development and of maintaining some degree of connection with Britain. Yet gradually a watershed was being crossed, as more and more stress was laid on the winning of national rights. Thus came the second phase, which dealt primarily with the achievement of autonomy in external affairs, and the motto of most of its authors might well have been, A Canadian Citizen I will Die.

Sometimes, it is true, these historians might welcome the emergence of the new British Commonwealth as the concomitant of Canada's advance to nationhood.[4] But generally they were less friendly to British influences, and the nationalist note was clear, as in the writings of J. W. Dafoe or O. D. Skelton. British influences, in short, were largely equated with imperial leading strings, and the more nationalistic writers were ever on guard against imperialist designs to enmesh pure young Canada in a web of power politics—though one might wonder why gentlemen so keenly perceptive of the harsh realities of power in the European world could not recognize, in fixing their watchful eye on the British menace, that, after 1918, at least, the fearsome British lion had become rather a straw-stuffed beast. Still, this preoccupation with straw men or straw lions may perhaps be explained by the fact that much of their writing was done amidst the somewhat unreal atmosphere of Mackenzie King's bold crusade of the 1920's for Canada's right to have no foreign policy. And these authors were often strongly Liberal in sympathies. At times they seemed to write as if Canadian

---

ments, for example, may not fit easily into a general school, though some aspects of their writings may suggest a possible affiliation. Then again, some authors may display elements of more than one school. In this regard, the imposing figure of G. M. Wrong seems to stand between the Britannic and Nationhood schools, and indeed suggests the transition from one to the other. Professor Wrong assuredly wrote with a consciousness of developing Canadian nationalism. But perhaps the "Britannic" element in his thought was well expressed in these words from an article of 1920 discussing the sometimes difficult advances made by Dominion nationalism during the First World War: "Yet in spite of this the British peoples were one. Probably we tend in smooth and easy days to underestimate the effects of the deep roots of unbroken tradition which nourish the life of a nation. The liberties of Canada have come, not without struggle, slowly from precedent to precedent based on parallel changes within Britain herself. It is the same in Australia. What these young states thus prize most in their own life is what Britain herself prizes most and it has involved no rupture of the long past or with the parent state. There is among all of them a continued unity in tradition and in political development." *Canadian Historical Review*, I, no. 1, "Canada and the Imperial War Cabinet," 23.

[4] For example, W. P. M. Kennedy. See particularly his many reviews of the 1920's, and annual review articles of the earlier 1930's, in the *Canadian Historical Review* on aspects of imperial constitutional law and Canada's relations therewith.

history was in essence a steady Liberal broadening-down of freedom to the ultimate end of national status—after which absolutely memorable History would come to a dead stop.[5]

Nevertheless the Political Nationhood group, first phase or second, did solid service in uncovering the process whereby Canada obtained the various attributes of self-government. Moreover, in stressing the theme of nationhood they were themselves expressing the basic truth that a society distinct from that of Britain had taken shape in Canada and was demanding recognition and the full right to manage its own affairs. As these historians, however, generally talked in political and constitutional terms, they did not effectively analyze the social, economic, and intellectual forces within North America which were creating a Canadian community increasingly conscious that it was far from being an overseas projection of Britain.

To fill this gap, a new school of historians began to take shape in the later 1920's, although it is important to note that its members were often closely related to the nationalist authors of the day. Indeed, this was nationalism in another sphere, seeking to demonstrate that Canadian desires for nationhood were rooted in the native North American environment: that Canadian institutions and viewpoints were not simply British, but were in their own way as American as those of the United States. The environment had done it. This, then, was the Environmentalist School, or North Americans All.

It was this group that built particularly on the concept of the frontier in North American history derived from Turner and his followers in the United States. The frontier, where man came most immediately into contact with the North American physical environ-

[5]See particularly J. W. Dafoe, *Laurier, a Study in Canadian Politics* (Toronto, 1922), and *Canada, an American Nation* (New York, 1935); and O. D. Skelton, *The Life and Letters of Sir Wilfrid Laurier* (2 vols., Toronto, 1921). See also, of course, the work of J. S. Ewart, who although a lawyer—as Dafoe was an editor, and Skelton became a civil servant—no less followed a nationalist historical approach in dealing with questions of autonomy. Writers of the young *Canadian Forum* "school," rather left of Liberalism, also expressed a deep suspicion of British imperial entanglements. (See the unpublished M.A. thesis by Margaret Prang at the University of Toronto, 1953, "Some Aspects of Political Radicalism in Canada between the Two World Wars.") Others less nationalist in tone but still notably concerned with Canada's developing autonomy were A. G. Dewey (*The Dominions and Diplomacy*, 2 vols., London, 1929) and R. M. Dawson (ed. and introd. to, *Development of Dominion Status, 1900–36*, Toronto, 1937). G. P. Glazebrook and F. H. Soward might also be mentioned as later "affiliates" of this school, but only in the sense that they did valuable work in its field of primary interest, the development of Canadian external relations, rather than that they carried on its earlier mood of eager nationalism.

ment, was the great seed-bed for the growth of a truly North American society. From the start, as the United States and Canada had spread across the continent, environmental influences that first began on the frontier had worked to shape a native American character different from that of the Old World, left far behind. Here was the key principle to be applied by Canadian environmentalist historians: that thanks to the continuous process of adaptation to the environment, an American content had steadily grown in Canada within external forms of government, society, or culture inherited from Britain or France.[6]

It followed that Canadian history could be most fruitfully compared to that of the United States in its essentially North American nature and course of development. In pursuing this promising theme, however, these writers took over the general approach and mood of Turner and company—the frontier and its agrarian population as emblematic of native democratic, progressive, perhaps even of "Good" forces in the history of the continent—rather than the precise frontier thesis, which received little direct application in Canada. Yet because that original thesis was so powerful in its impact and so pervasive in its influence, it requires examination here; although, admittedly, the subject is hardly a new one.[7]

II

Turner had held in his frontier thesis that "the greatest formative influence" in American history had been the long existence of "the open frontier, the hither edge of free land," continually moving westwards.[8] The conditions of frontier society had determined the character of western institutions, and these in turn had reacted on

[6]The work of this school will be discussed in detail in subsequent pages, but for now let it be said that, at one time or another, its membership might be held to include W. B. Munro, F. H. Underhill, W. N. Sage, A. R. M. Lower, F. Landon, A. S. Morton, and A. L. Burt. Qualifications will of course be necessary, but at any rate the above authors made good use of frontier-environmentalist concepts in various writings, whatever else they may also have done. Furthermore, J. B. Brebner worked in the environmentalist vein to some extent, and might be regarded as an "affiliate" of this school during much of the 1930's, while W. L. Morton might be deemed a somewhat later affiliate. It should be plain that no tight determinism is intended in thus naming these authors, nor, on the whole, did they display any. Yet the influence of environmentalism upon them may well be remarked, and hence it seems instructive to try to class them in this fashion for the purposes of this paper, even though many of them might subsequently move on to different perspectives when the peak of the Environmentalist School had passed.

[7]See M. Zaslow, "The Frontier Hypothesis in Recent Historiography," *Canadian Historical Review*, XXIX, no. 2, 1948, for a fairly recent examination.

[8]Turner's thesis was first embodied in his paper, "The Significance of the Frontier in American History," read before the American Historical Association in 1893, and

the East. Out of the frontier, in fact, had come American individualism, democracy, inventiveness, coarseness, and idealism. Turner wrote that the seeds of American democracy were not carried to the New World in the *Mayflower* but sprang up out of the native forest. The effect of the frontier was to make Americans out of Europeans. In brief, the West was the true America, that ever taught the populous but effete East the American way of life.

This was environmental determinism at its most forthright. The wilderness and the men it produced had made America. Defenders of Turner might claim that he had not proposed a frontier hypothesis as the only key to American history, but it was widely seized upon as the true explanation, especially as its nationalist and romantic implications gripped the American imagination.[9] Its effects may still be found today, on different cultural levels in the United States. Indeed, it may not be irrelevant to note that Hollywood, that lowest common denominator of the American mind where myths are mass-produced, still pours forth a flood of highly technicoloured Westerns each purporting to touch the very soul of America, as some pioneer rugged individualist with iron hands and blazing guns "carves out an empire" for the nation at various points west, while Indians in their thousands from Central Casting Office go down before the onward march of democracy.

Of course Hollywood is a far cry from the academic world of history, and here there have been repeated and detailed criticisms of the frontier thesis as applied in the United States. Nevertheless the stimulus it gave to environmentalist—at times even isolationist—study of American history remained a powerful one. Moreover, a broad survey of the opinions of American historians made a little over a decade ago revealed that the majority would still accept the frontier thesis, with qualifications, although the trend seemed to be turning against it.[10] In this trend were men like Carleton Hayes, who asked, concerning the American frontier, "frontier of what?" and answered that America was essentially the western edge of European civilization. Accordingly, its story could be read as part

---

ultimately reprinted in his *Frontier in American History* (New York, 1920). I am indebted here to the succinct description of Turnerism in G. F. G. Stanley's paper, "Western Canada and the Frontier Thesis," *Canadian Historical Association Report*, 1940, 105. See also Zaslow, "The Frontier Hypothesis," 154–5.

[9]See F. L. Paxson, "A Generation of the Frontier Hypothesis, 1893–1932," *Pacific Historical Review*, II, no. 1, 1933, and also H. N. Smith, *Virgin Land: The American West as Symbol and Myth* (Cambridge, 1950), especially the concluding chapter on Turner.

[10]G. W. Pierson, "American Historians and the Frontier Hypothesis in 1941," *Wisconsin Magazine of History*, XXVI, nos. 1 and 2, 1942.

of the expansion of Europe; and its culture and institutions should be studied not solely in national isolation as native products, but rather as elements transferred from Europe, adjusting—no doubt—to a somewhat different environment.[11]

Dixon Ryan Fox also pursued this theme of transfer, finding that the ideas and institutions transmitted from Europe bulked far larger in American development than any modifications of them or new contributions made on this side of the Atlantic. He observed, in fact, that ideas and institutions had steadily been carried west *to* the frontier, and considered that the East had far more shaped the West in America than *vice versa*—that the real story of the United States was the progressive turning of pioneer Wests into developed Easts.[12] Further in this vein, Arthur M. Schlesinger Jr. sought to demonstrate that the upsurge of Jacksonian Democracy, long regarded as the very incarnation and triumph of the free farming frontier, was instead far more strongly based amid the urban masses of the East.[13]

The frontiersmen among American historians have, however, struck back. One of them, W. P. Webb, has recently launched a most dazzling counter-attack on all fronts by proclaiming that the whole expansion of Europe since 1500 was one "Age of the Great Frontier."[14] He contends that most of modern Western European civilization as we know it, with its characteristic capitalism, democracy, and individualism, is the product of world frontiers that opened up to Europe when its peoples began to go adventuring across the oceans. He speaks of a four-hundred-year frontier boom, now ended, when Europe grew rich and developed the twin luxuries of freedom and the all-important individual, a boom that resulted from the "windfalls" of vast natural resources that were found in the empty Americas, Australasia, and South Africa. Europe became a dominating metropolis—a word we shall return to later—organizing, controlling, and exploiting these tremendous overseas frontiers, but in consequence having its development moulded by them.

How does all this relate to Canadian history? To some extent there have been similar stages in the use of the frontier interpretation, though these, indeed, might overlap. In the first stage, there

[11]C. J. H. Hayes, "The American Frontier—Frontier of What?" *American Historical Review*, LI, no. 2, 1946.

[12]D. R. Fox, *Ideas in Motion* (New York, 1935). See also his introduction to *Sources of Culture in the Middle West* (D. R. Fox, ed., New York, 1934).

[13]A. M. Schlesinger, Jr., *The Age of Jackson* (Boston, 1945).

[14]W. P. Webb, *The Great Frontier* (Boston, 1953).

were stimulating applications of frontierist themes and concepts to the Canadian half of the North American environment, seen most clearly perhaps in W. N. Sage's paper of 1928, "Some Aspects of the Frontier in Canadian History." This treated Canadian expansion across the continent as an integral part of a total North American frontier movement that ignored the international boundary.[15] Then there were the valuable investigations of F. H. Underhill into the nature of Canadian political parties, and especially the Clear Grit Liberal movement directed by George Brown and the Toronto *Globe*. With regard to Canadian parties, Professor Underhill traced their development according to conflicts between western agrarian areas and eastern business interests, in sound Turnerian fashion (1935).[16] With regard to the Clear Grits, he saw them as "an expression of the 'frontier' in Canadian politics" (1927).[17] E. H. Oliver applied frontierism to Canadian religious development, and in his *Winning the Frontier* (1930) depicted the Canadian churches as being moulded by a frontier environment.[18] Somewhat later A. S. Morton emphasized the dominant power of the environment in the extension of settlement into the Prairie West (1938).[19] And

[15]*Canadian Historical Association Report*, 1928. See also M. L. Hansen and J. B. Brebner, *The Mingling of the Canadian and American Peoples* (Toronto, 1940), for a general integration of Canadian settlement into the whole theme of North American frontier expansion. Professor Brebner also followed this approach in his essay, "The Survival of Canada," in *Essays in Canadian History Presented to G. M. Wrong* (R. Flenley, ed., Toronto, 1939). In this he ascribed Canadian survival to the cross-pulls of American sectionalism and to the British connection rather than "predominantly to Canadian resistance," so that the emergence of a Canadian nation was largely an externally produced modification of the general North American process of settlement: for, ". . . to the student of population the settled regions of Canada, with the great exception of Quebec, appear on the whole to be outward projections of the settled regions of the United States . . . rather than interlocked units of a separate people which has systematically expanded its occupation from Atlantic to Pacific" (272–3).

[16]F. H. Underhill, "The Development of National Political Parties in Canada," *Canadian Historical Review*, XVI, no. 4, 1935. See also W. B. Munro, *American Influences on Canadian Government* (Toronto, 1929), for the influence of frontier environment on party organization and politics.

[17]F. H. Underhill, "Some Aspects of Upper Canadian Radical Opinion in the Decade before Confederation," *Canadian Historical Association Report*, 1927, 47. See also G. W. Brown, "The Grit Party and the Great Reform Convention of 1859," *Canadian Historical Review*, XVI, no. 3, 1935.

[18]E. H. Oliver, *The Winning of the Frontier* (Toronto, 1930).

[19]A. S. Morton, *History of Prairie Settlement* (Canadian Frontiers of Settlement, VII, part 1, Toronto, 1938). See also, but to lesser extent because of its largely "pre-settlement" theme, A. S. Morton, *A History of the Canadian West to 1870–1* (Toronto, 1939). The attention paid to environmental forces at this period is well suggested by the whole Canadian Frontiers of Settlement series of the later thirties, a nine-volume project under the Canadian Pioneer Problems Committee, begun in 1934.

A. L. Burt effectively used a frontier interpretation to show how the people of New France were shaped by North American forces to become truly an indigenous people, not just a seeming copy of Old World "feudal" France (1940).[20]

In the second stage, there came criticisms and modifications of the frontier interpretation, although the environmentalist emphasis was still much in evidence.[21] A. R. M. Lower noted in a paper of 1930, "The Origins of Democracy in Canada," that "There can be little question but that American democracy had a forest birth." Yet he went on to assert that frontier equality might not result in political democracy unless "theoretical positions as to its nature" had already been projected into the frontier environment. In Canada's case, the egalitarian conditions of pioneer life had interacted with traditions brought from across the Atlantic; and Canadian democracy had developed more slowly than American because of Canada's briefer, more limited frontier experience, its stronger attachments to the Old World, and the long-enduring, overriding power of the imperial authority in government.[22] Nevertheless, despite this recognition of non-environmental, transferred influences, Professor Lower, in his *Colony to Nation* (1946) continued to stress the power of the New World "to change old institutions and give

[20]A. L. Burt, "The Frontier in the History of New France," *Canadian Historical Association Report*, 1940. See also his *Short History of Canada for Americans* (Minneapolis, 1942), 23–31. In a more recent work, however, his presidential address before the Canadian Historical Association, "Broad Horizons" (*Report*, 1950), Professor Burt sought a broadening of approach, beyond the continent of North America, to take in Canada's background in imperial history. And he noted that wider views in history had largely been replaced in Canada after the First World War by a heavy concentration on developments in the narrowly Canadian scene, thanks to "the rising tide of Canadian nationalism"—a statement which might well sum up the whole environmentalist phase. See also his study, *The United States, Great Britain, and British North America from the Revolution to the Establishment of Peace after the War of 1812* (Toronto, 1940), which rejects a frontier expansionist view of the causes of the War of 1812, stressing rather the maritime clashes between Britain and the United States.

[21]Examples of criticism of the application of the frontier thesis to Canada are J. L. McDougall, "The Frontier School and Canadian History," *Canadian Historical Association Report*, 1929, and G. F. G. Stanley, "Western Canada and the Frontier Thesis."

[22]*Canadian Historical Association Report*, 1930, 66–70. "It must therefore be a modified or adapted version of the [Turner] thesis which can be fitted to Canada" (66). See also Professor Lower's paper, "Some Neglected Aspects of Canadian History," *Canadian Historical Association Report*, 1929, 67–8. These articles indicate that from the start, so to speak, the author was concerned about the weight to be given to tradition and political structure as well as to environment in explaining the course of Canadian history.

them new form and spirit."[23] North American democracy, he re-iterated, was "forest-born." In short, though this was modification, environmentalism sprung from the frontier concept still remained strong.

In the third stage, as in the United States, new emphasis was given to the role of eastern rather than western forces in Canada, to urban interests and to the dominating power of the organizing, controlling metropolis. Thus Professor Underhill, for example, noted in 1946 that the original frontier agrarianism of the Clear Grits had subsequently been qualified by urban and business leadership intro-duced to the party by George Brown and other Toronto worthies.[24] And Professor Lower in his same *Colony to Nation* paid marked attention to the economic power wielded by metropolitan centres like Montreal and London, which, he made clear, did much to affect the course of events in raw Canadian settlements.[25] On another tack, Professor Fred Landon, in describing the frontier era in western Ontario, gave chief place to the transmitted influence of American democratic ideas and practices rather than to actual frontier conditions in forming the outlook of the pioneer com-munity.[26] But this only pushed the influence of the environment one stage back, to patterns of life worked out in the former frontier states below the Great Lakes. In any case it was evident that, despite qualifications and shifts of emphasis, environmentalism was still flourishing in Canadian history.

Still, it should be plain from this discussion that Canadian en-vironmentalists did not generally follow any rigid frontier dogma and did show regard for other than native or western forces in analysing Canadian developments. After all, in a country which

[23]*Colony to Nation* (Toronto, 1946), 48–9. See also J. B. Brebner, "Canadian and North American History," *Canadian Historical Association Report*, 1931, in which the author noted the "identities of contour between Canadian history and North American" produced by the continental environment (42), but also remarked on points of difference, for example, in the administration of justice, where "The frontier theory of North American history, that enthusiastic elaboration of Prof. F. J. Turner's reasonable suggestions, obviously will not serve" (45).

[24]F. H. Underhill, "Some Reflections on the Liberal Tradition in Canada," *Canadian Historical Association Report*, 1946.

[25]*Colony to Nation*, 198–200. See also Professor Lower's *North American Assault on the Canadian Forest* (Toronto, 1938), in which organizing, dominating, metro-politan economic forces are shown in action in the forest environment. Another significant volume bearing on the relation of frontier areas to urban business interests is his earlier *Settlement and the Forest Frontier in Eastern Canada* (Canadian Frontiers of Settlement, IX, part 1, Toronto, 1936).

[26]Fred Landon, *Western Ontario and the American Frontier* (Toronto, 1941).

had obviously maintained many transatlantic ties and long continued as a colony there could not be as strong an assertion as in
the United States of a separate North American growth in isolation
from the world. And yet there was an inclination for environmentalists to see as much as possible of the history of Canada in
terms of common North American experience in driving back the
wilds—to suggest that the really important features in Canadian
development had in truth been "forest-born"; in other words, that
the various Wests had been the principal source of transforming
energy and of national progress, in which they had pulled along
and supported the conservative, exploitative East.

There was, moreover, a certain tendency to fix values. Thus
pioneer society, the West, and simple farmers became virtuous and
forward-looking to the beholder, while town society, the East, and
un-simple business men became selfish and reactionary. There
might be an element of truth here, but moral overtones somewhat
coloured the picture, so that western farmers who wanted free trade
established in their interests were Good, while eastern business men
who wanted a protective tariff enacted in theirs were Evil. Similarly,
the West appeared as the true home of Canadianism, while the
East, which worked out a distinctive Canadian economic nationalism in railway and tariff policy, was hardly Canada at all. No doubt
powerful eastern business interests fattened themselves considerably
through these arrangements. But could environmentalists properly
become moral about business elements adjusting themselves to
problems of the environment in their own way?

In sum, Canadian environmentalists frequently displayed the
compelling mood of the frontier school, with its moral implications
of a struggle between sound native democratic forces and elements
that clung to privilege, exploitation, and empty Old-World forms.
In so doing they often oversimplified a conflict between West and
East, or better, between pioneer agrarian interests and exploitative
urban centres. As a result, major Canadian movements for political
change might be viewed too narrowly in the light of frontierism.
For example, Upper Canadian radicalism of the 1830's, Clear Grit
Liberalism of the mid-century, and Progressivism of the 1920's
might all be explained in terms of the upsurge of the then new-
est West, as western forces of pioneer individualism launched
crusades against privilege and urban business domination.[27] Yet it

27Note, for example, W. L. Morton, "Direct Legislation and the Origins of the
Progressive Movement," *Canadian Historical Review*, XXV, no. 3, 1944: "It [Pro-
gressivism] was the latest upsurge of agrarian and frontier democracy" (279).

could also be shown that Mackenzie radicalism was probably more influenced by the working model of American political democracy and the ideas of British radicalism; that Clear Grittism was closely organized about the rising urban centre of Toronto; and that Western Progressivism was not based on self-sufficient pioneer farmers but on organized grain specialists engaged in a highly complex kind of agricultural business, whose goals involved not the triumph of individualism but the replacement of a set of unfavourable government controls centred in the tariff with another represented by Wheat Boards and government provision of major services.

Furthermore, it might well be a result of frontierism, sprung as it was from the mid-western heart of the continent, that a viewpoint characteristic of mid-western isolationism often appeared among environmentalist writers in Canada. Their view of the environment, lik Turner's, was primarily continental. Thus it tended to neglect the influence of the seas beyond, the "maritime environment" that had always tied the continent to Europe. Canada might be treated as a northern extension of certain continental physiographic provinces, without due consideration of geographic and historic forces that had from the beginning of white penetration made this country an east-to-west projection from Europe. And logically it would follow that geography—in the continental sense only—had shaped Canada as a number of disparate American regions, held out of the American republic by mainly emotional forces and by the chance of history: in short, a loose grouping of less well-favoured, somewhat backward, American states. A rather paradoxical basis, this, for the nationalism environmentalists usually professed.

However, it is worth repeating that leading contemporary historians who have been referred to here in connection with the vigorous environmentalist phase of Canadian history have themselves, in more recent writings, not only shown awareness of the shortcomings of interpretations stemming from frontierism but have also done much to reconsider and to correct them. Nor, certainly, have their ideas ceased to develop beyond this one approach. None the less it may be hazarded that the effects of frontierist teachings remain strong today in suggesting for Canadian history, and doubtless for its readers, certain stereotypes about the dynamic West and the torpid East, and about the nature of Canada as a more restricted, backward version of the American model to the south. And frontierism may still leave a tendency to overvalue the influence of native North American forces and the material environment, and a tendency to undervalue forces transferred from Europe and the non-

material environment: that of ideas, traditions and institutions. Yet
these latter factors were particularly important in a portion of North
America that did not undergo a revolutionary upheaval, emotional
as well as political, to break ties with Europe, and which continued
to place a special premium on the word "British" as applied to
institutions and ideas. In fact, it is these very things which chiefly
mark off the development of Canada from that of the United States.
They give validity to the study of a separate Canadian history, one
which is not just a counterpart of United States history in having a
similar North American content.

Accordingly, while in no way underrating the very great contributions which frontierism and environmentalism have made to
the understanding of Canada as a part of North America, it does
seem necessary to look for a wider framework for Canadian history.
But this, indeed, was already taking shape while the frontier
interpretation was being usefully applied, and to a certain extent
grew out of it, as an examination will show.

III

This next framework was in some ways a qualified version of environmentalism and in others the frontier concept reversed. It has
appeared in most explicit form in the writings of D. G. Creighton,
particularly in his *Commercial Empire of the St. Lawrence* (1938)
and *Dominion of the North* (1944), but its foundations were laid
in earlier works by H. A. Innis which broke rich new ground in
Canadian economic history, notably *A History of the Canadian
Pacific Railway* (1923) and *The Fur Trade in Canada* (1930).
These studies of major Canadian economic enterprises, which were
essentially great systems of continent-wide communications, pointed
the way to a new general interpretation of Canadian history that
would be forcefully developed by Professor Creighton.

His approach, in fact, has been said to establish a "Laurentian
School" of Canadian historiography, since it largely rests on the idea
that the long St. Lawrence water route and its connections across
the continent became the basis of an extensive communications
system around which Canada itself took shape. The commercial
empire of the St. Lawrence, the broad domain of Montreal, first
flung a Canadian fur trade across the continent, then competed
vigorously with New York and the American seaboard through
canal and railway enterprises for control of the trade of the mid-
western heartlands of America, and finally built a new economic
dominion across the northwestern plains to the Pacific that was, in

fact, the Dominion of Canada. It followed that the existence of a separate Canada was not just a fortuitous result of the American Revolution, of French determination to survive, nor of Loyalist emotional resolves to "stay British"—despite the hard facts of the environment—nor again of the mere continuance of the imperial tie. It was also rooted in powerful factors of geography and commerce that underlay the whole Canadian development.

This, in a sense, was environmentalism, since the St. Lawrence was as real a feature of the North American environment as the North American forest, and a good deal more permanent. Environmentalists had stressed before that the main natural lines of North American geography ran north and south, linking the regions of Canada more effectively with their United States counterparts below the border than with their Canadian neighbours to east and west. But the St. Lawrence, the Great Lakes, the Saskatchewan, and the Fraser traced lines across the continent that were quite as natural; and, as the writings of Professors Innis and Creighton indicated, they made possible the east-to-west linking of Canadian regions from the earliest days of the fur trade, as communications spread by the lakes and river valleys from sea to sea. Perhaps we could even call this the Waterways School, especially since it made clear that the environment did not stop short at the Atlantic edge of North America. For the St. Lawrence system that funnelled traffic from the continental interior out to the sea was closely connected with British finance and markets across the waters in an east-west trading network that thus reached halfway around the world.[28]

[28]The growing emphasis on "maritime factors" in Canadian and indeed North American history was a major development of the 1940's that extended and greatly recast environmentalist thinking, or—as it might also be put—marked the transition to a newer, wider interpretation of Canadian history. Perhaps the growing recognition of "extra-continental" forces could be linked to the impact of the Second World War, which sharply checked isolationist tendencies in Canadian thought, as the outside world was borne in upon it: a different result from that of the First World War, already noted, which enhanced a rather inward-looking nationalism. The significance of broad strategic factors, many of imperial or at least extra-continental origin, was newly observed in Canadian history, largely owing to the rise of a "military" school, if the name be permitted, in which the rather neglected military and naval side of Canadian development were dealt with by such historians as C. P. Stacey, G. S. Graham, and G. N. Tucker. On the primarily economic side, H. A. Innis' *The Cod Fisheries* (Toronto, 1940) was of critical importance in showing the Atlantic not as a dividing waste of waters but as a linking network of waterways that served an international and intercontinental economy. As Dr. J. T. Shotwell said in its preface, "it extends the frontiers of North America over a vast area that we have never thought of before as constituting a part—and a fundamental part—of the continent." In more general terms than just the economic, G. W. Brown had answered

Yet the Laurentian interpretation did not mean just a new emphasis on material environmentalism, since it also revealed that this huge communications and transport system could transfer immigrants, ideas, and impulses in one direct channel from Britain deep into the heart of the continent. As a result, the Ontario frontier of the earlier nineteenth century might actually be in closer contact with the sea and the mind of Europe than were the mid-western regions of the United States, more isolated behind the Appalachian barrier in a Mississippi Valley world of their own.

The Laurentian School, however, tended to go even further, and to reverse the earlier environmentalist position in this respect: it looked not from the forest-born frontiers for its perspective of Canadian history but from developing eastern centres of commerce and industry. Indeed, it primarily studied the effects of the East on the West, and largely regarded business men and conservative urban political elements as agents of national expansion who might well be more far-sighted in their outlook than were their agrarian opponents. Here then was a metropolitan rather than a frontier viewpoint. Moreover, this Laurentian view could be effectively linked with the monumental studies of H. A. Innis on the organization of the staple products trade of broad North American areas through costly and complex transport systems controlled in large urban centres.[29] The result was virtually to establish "metropolitanism" in Canadian historiography, the study of the role of metropolitan forces in this country, a vitalizing approach that may yet undergo considerable development.

---

the question of whether the Americas had a common history by asserting that they had, as integral parts of an Atlantic world ("Have the Americas a Common History? A Canadian View," *Canadian Historical Review*, XXIII, no. 2, 1942). And J. B. Brebner, in closing and climaxing the great Carnegie series of studies in Canadian-American relations with his *North Atlantic Triangle* (Toronto, 1945), had found, strikingly enough, that his original plan to "set forth the interplay between Canada and the United States" had had to be extended to take in transatlantic influences stemming from Britain—and thus his significant title. His book was of double importance. Not only did it markedly reveal the transfer of forces and culture across the Atlantic lake and around the great triangle of Britain, the United States, and Canada; it also indicated that a massive set of studies on Canadian-American relations, whose very inception in the early thirties expressed the then-current concern with North American environmentalism, had ended in the forties in a new awareness of forces that reached far beyond the continental limits. Certainly a new approach to Canadian and North American historiography was taking shape.

[29]See, as well as works of Professor Innis already cited, *Problems of Staple Production in Canada* (Toronto, 1933); *Settlement and the Mining Frontier* (Canadian Frontiers of Settlement, IX, part 2, Toronto, 1936); "Transportation as a Factor in Canadian Economic History," *Proceedings of the Canadian Political Science Association*, 1931; and "Significant Factors in Canadian Economic Development," *Canadian Historical Review*, XVIII, no. 4, 1937.

Metropolitanism is at root a socio-economic concept that has already seen some application in Canadian history. As mentioned earlier, Professor Lower has made use of it in *Colony to Nation*, and elsewhere as well,[30] but it has been most closely applied in D. C. Masters' work, *The Rise of Toronto, 1850–1890* (1947).[31] In this he traced the rise of the city to a position of metropolitan dominance over Ontario, while at the same time it entered into vigorous competition with Montreal business interests for control of a broader Canadian hinterland. Toronto's climb to metropolitan stature is an instructive particular theme in Canadian history, but the rise of the metropolis in general is one of the most striking features of modern Western society. Briefly this implies the emergence of a city of outstanding size to dominate not only its surrounding countryside but other cities and their countrysides, the whole area being organized by the metropolis, through control of communications, trade, and finance, into one economic and social unit that is focussed on the metropolitan "centre of dominance" and through it trades with the world.[32] Political activity, too, may often become centred on the metropolis.

London and New York are of course the classic examples of modern metropolitanism. But the metropolitan relationship is a chain, almost a feudal chain of vassalage, wherein one city may stand tributary to a bigger centre and yet be the metropolis of a sizable region of its own. Thus, for example, Winnipeg is Montreal's subsidiary but is the metropolis of a large area of the prairie West. The Toronto metropolis is a subsidiary of both New York and Montreal, while Canada's main metropolitan centre, Montreal, has traditionally been bound to London. These facts are not new in

[30]See note 25 above. Also, for a stimulating outline of the roles of Canadian metropolitan centres, Montreal, Toronto and Vancouver, and their competition for "hinterlands," see Professor Lower's essay, "Geographical Determinants in Canadian History," in *Essays Presented to G. M. Wrong*, 245–51. Indeed, he discerns in the whole pattern of Canadian economic development, "the characteristic expression of the staple trade, the metropolitan-hinterland relationship" ("Two Ways of Life: The Primary Antithesis of Canadian History," *Canadian Historical Association Report*, 1943, 13).

[31]Professor Masters here applies the concept of economic metropolitan dominance put forward by N. S. B. Gras in his *Introduction to Economic History* (New York, 1922) though he extends it as well to social and cultural fields. According to Gras, a city rises to metropolitan dominance over a hinterland region through four stages: first, it creates a well-organized marketing system for the whole area; second, manufacturing develops in the metropolis or the hinterland; third, there is an active programme of transportation development; and fourth, a mature financial system is constructed to provide for the trade both with the hinterland and with the outside world (See preface to *The Rise of Toronto*, Toronto, 1947).

[32]See C. A. Dawson and W. E. Gettys, *An Introduction to Sociology* (New York, 1948), 154–71.

themselves; but when it is remembered that the metropolitan pattern includes not only economic ties but social and cultural associations also, then many effective lines of inquiry may present themselves. For example, one might suggest that the survival of British customs sometimes noted in the English-speaking ruling class of Montreal, or Toronto's split personality, whereby it strives both to be a minor New York and to maintain its "British" character, may be comprehended through the weighing of various metropolitan connections and influences in these cities' history.

At present, however, the chief point to observe is that the rise of metropolitanism is the other side of the coin to frontier expansion. One may speak of the constant expansion of the frontier, or of the constant extension of the metropolitan power that is pushing out the frontier. What Webb called the "Age of the Great Frontier," might just as well be called the "Age of the Great Metropolis," when western Europe in general, by spreading out its system of communications and commerce, organized the world about itself. The age of this great European metropolis has passed away. Its predominant focus, London, has yielded in primacy of economic power to New York—though now there is no one main world metropolitan region, since, despite the rise of North America, Europe still maintains a vast overseas economic network, while a far-flung separate trading system is emerging in the Communist-dominated world.

Returning to the frontier itself, one might say that it is developed by a metropolitan centre of dominance which supplies its capital, organizes its communications and transport, and markets its products. The frontier's culture, too, originally stems from a metropolitan community; at root, learning and ideas radiate from there —and thus is Turner answered. True, there may be frontier religious movements, but these begin with preachers going out to the frontier and end in the focusing of the sect on the city.[33] The economic and cultural metropolitan processes go hand in hand, as newspapers, books, and men of education spread from the centre. Frontiers may often supply grievances for political movements. Urban centres as often supply the intellectual leadership; so that frontier demands take form at the hands of urban journalists and professional men.

It may be seen when this analysis is carried through that the frontier, far from being essentially independent and self-reliant, is in the largest sense a dependent. It constantly requires metropolitan

[33]See S. D. Clark, *Church and Sect in Canada* (Toronto, 1949), especially 90–173.

aid and control, though by the same token it may come to resent and resist it. Frontier protest movements are a natural accompaniment of the extension of metropolitan power into new areas. The dynamic, organizing, hard-pressing forces of metropolitanism bring reaction on themselves. This may occur either at moments when the frontier as such is rapidly expanding, and full of problems of adjustment, or when it is actually declining; that is, becoming organized into a more mature and integrated region with a new metropolitan centre of its own, which hopes to wrest control of the local economy away from the older centre, and therefore gives voice and leadership to a regional protest movement.

How does this pattern fit Canadian history? No good historian would try to make it fit too exactly: if we reject a frontier determinism we should hardly replace it with a metropolitan determinism. Still, there may be an approach here as instructive for Canadian historiography as the frontier interpretation was in its day. For example, one might examine the unrest in Upper Canada in the 1830's, when this frontier area was rapidly expanding with the tide of British immigration, as a result of the vigorous extension of powerful business interests into a broad new domain, and of the spread of educated men and stimulating ideas from older communities, displayed notably in the rising power of the press and the journalist on the Upper Canada scene. On the other hand, the Clear Grit movement of the 1850's would appear as the organizing of the maturing western community around Toronto, the rising young metropolis, in a common campaign against the domination of the region by Montreal, the older centre. In this campaign Toronto supplied both intellectual leadership, in the form of the *Globe*, and strong party direction, in the form of George Brown and other wealthy and prominent business or professional men: the urban element was critically important. And as for Western Progressivism in the 1920's, was it not bound up with the rise of Winnipeg as a prairie metropolitan centre, was not a good deal of intellectual leadership centred in that city, and is there not evidence that here was a maturing western community now ready to contest outside metropolitan domination on a large scale?[34]

34W. L. Morton, in his admirable recent study, *The Progressive Party in Canada* (Toronto, 1950), has written of the whole Progressive movement in strongly western environmental terms. Yet while interpreting Progressivism in the light of a frontier agrarian background, he has also showed awareness of the impact of metropolitan forces throughout. See also the foreword to this volume by S. D. Clark, noting that this western sectional protest ended by "becoming accommodated to the power structure of the metropolitan-federal system" (ix).

Metropolitanism can be seen operating even more clearly in Canadian history where there are no frontiers of actual settlement to block the view, so to speak, and by their undoubted colour and liveliness rather steal the centre of the stage. In the Canadian fur trade, from earliest French times on, the role of the dominant organizing metropolis is plain: Montreal and Quebec the metropolitan centres for the posts of the whole fur-trading West, Paris and later London the metropolis for these Canadian towns. On the Canadian lumbering and mining frontiers, in our present northern expansion, the directing, extending, organizing, and exploiting functions of metropolitan interests are evident once more. In fact, metropolitanism has shown itself even more clearly in Canadian development than in American, precisely because we have had far less fertile acreage for agricultural settlement than has the United States. Hence the agrarian frontier of the sort that Turner described has played proportionately less part in our history. This, then, is a distinctive attribute of Canada's own version of the North American story.

Furthermore, in Canada, with its small population heavily concentrated in certain areas, metropolitan influences have had a particularly free sweep. The United States, of course, has much bigger metropolitan cities like Chicago, Philadelphia, and New York. But it also has many more large centres, each organizing its own region, though all ultimately subordinate to New York. Canada, however, has only three first-ranking metropolitan centres today: Montreal, the greatest, Vancouver, which by organizing effective communications has extended its hinterland eastward into the prairies, and Toronto, which controls wealthy southern Ontario and is steadily advancing its empire in the mining North. In Canada, therefore, metropolitan power is in comparison to the United States more directly centralized and more immediately apparent.

Historically speaking, the functioning of metropolitanism may do more to explain the course of Canadian history than concepts of frontierism borrowed from the United States and set forth before the significance of the modern metropolis was clear. For example, the greater conservatism of Canada as compared to the United States may be read as a mark of the much stronger influence exercised in this country by conservative-minded eastern urban centres —which were certainly far removed from any impulses of forest democracy. Moreover, the stronger influence of British ideas and institutions—and even of colonialism—must have been fostered in Canada by its long and close focusing on the British metropolis itself. Finally, the fact that Canada has pioneered not so much in democracy as in the large-scale combination of public and private interests to overcome the problems raised by a difficult environment, again suggests the greater power throughout Canadian history of the forces seeking to organize communication systems and extend commerce. One might well say that the building of the C.P.R. so far ahead of settlement, and Macdonald's policies of economic nationalism in general, were plain manifestations of the power of metropolitan influences in Canadian politics. And many other instances might also be brought to mind.[35]

It could be objected with regard to some of the foregoing examples that applying a metropolitan interpretation only restates old problems in somewhat different terms. It may be so: but what is particularly needed is a restatement, a new perspective that may disclose new vistas and produce new patterns for Canadian history. At any rate, frontierism, along with earlier schools and approaches, has had its use and its day. Environmentalism needs recasting, and is being recast. The metropolitan approach largely recognizes what is already going on in Canadian historiography and provides a new framework—one which pays heed both to the distinctive features of the history of this country and to a notable modern phenomenon, the rise of metropolitanism all around the world.

[35]It has been said by J. B. Brebner that "the most substantial Canadian nationalism in time of peace has been economic nationalism" ("Canadianism," *Canadian Historical Association Report*, 1940, 8), and others, such as W. S. MacNutt, have echoed that view (see his letter to the editors of the *Canadian Historical Review*, XXXIV, no. 1, 1953, 108). Since economic nationalism is pre-eminently the result of metropolitan forces, it might appear that the way to the "national" heart of Canadian development, if that is a desirable goal, lies not through the frontiers of field and forest, where the environmentalists sought it, but rather through the metropolitan approach.

The British Conquest:
Canadian Social Scientists and the
Fate of the *Canadiens*

MICHEL BRUNET

SOCIAL SCIENTISTS have the task of describing how human societies are built, how they develop, how they are arrested in their development, how they disintegrate, how they vanish. Such an undertaking is not an easy one. It requires long research, and much hard and fresh thinking about man's behaviour. Unfortunately, social sciences are still in their infancy. This field of knowledge has always been and is still neglected. For centuries, most social scientists were mere defenders of the *status quo*. They were entrusted with the job of vindicating the ruling classes to which they belonged or whose servants they were. Only a few thinkers did sincerely try to meditate upon the motives and interests which influence human history. Some reformers did unmask the false dogmas upon which the social order of their time rested. They were looked at with scorn, fear, or hostility in official and academic circles. One always takes the risk of being persecuted or ignored when one dares to question the social and political conceptions of the dominant minority.

We are now in the second half of the twentieth century. In the natural sciences, man has freed himself of all the fallacies which formerly impeded the extension of his knowledge of material things. Every day new frontiers of learning are opened to man's inquiry. But in the social sciences there has been little progress because too many social scientists have satisfied themselves with repeating the commonplaces, platitudes, and watchwords of past generations. They have not gone beyond the romantic period of the nineteenth century. Their vocabulary is a Victorian one. Others have spent their time writing long and dull monographic studies on minor topics and have missed the fundamental questions of their craft. Were they afraid to

*The Gray Lecture delivered at the University of Toronto, October 31, 1958.

Reprinted from *Canadian Historical Review*, XL (2), June, 1959

challenge the social creeds of their time and to contest the validity of their forefathers' ideology? Was the power of the ruling class so overwhelming that they have felt compelled to keep silent? Perhaps the majority have been the unconscious victims of social conformity.

In any case, the result is that we live in a world we do not understand. We are almost powerless to meet the problems of our industrialized and urbanized society. Social scientists must reconsider their frame of reference if they want to make a real, scientific, attempt to explain the political, economic, and social evolution of the Atlantic world from the Renaissance to our confused contemporary age. A new approach is needed, and the need is urgent.

There are many proofs of the social scientists' failures and shortcomings. It is not my intention to draw up an inventory. I shall confine myself to an historical and sociological problem which I have long studied: what has actually been the historical evolution of the French-Canadian collectivity since the British Conquest and occupation of the St. Lawrence valley, and how have four generations of social scientists interpreted this historical fact?

With the help of France, and under the direction of their natural leaders, the *Canadiens* had organized a colonial society in North America. They had the legitimate ambition of developing alone and for their own profit the St. Lawrence valley. For a century and a half, they succeeded in maintaining their separateness and their collective freedom.

Being too weak to keep for themselves the northern half of the continent, the *Canadiens* were defeated, conquered, and occupied. Many of their leaders, having realized that their interests as a ruling class were in jeopardy under a foreign domination, decided to emigrate. The mass of the people could not follow them and had no choice but to submit to the British invaders who now ruled the colony. French Canada could no longer rely on its mother country whose support it vitally needed to grow normally. A colonial nation is always the offspring of a metropolis devoted to its progress. Deprived of this help, the *Canadiens* were left to their own resources which were very limited. Their new lay leaders had no influence in politics and business. Their priests became their principal spokesmen, yet the collaboration of the clergy was necessary to the British authorities and they skilfully managed to keep it. As a collectivity, the *Canadiens* were doomed to an anaemic survival. One must never forget that to survive is not to live.

Canada now belonged to a new collectivity. Having taken into their hands political and economic control of the St. Lawrence valley, the

British administrators and merchants—the cleverer among them—
wanted to establish a prosperous colonial nation of their own stock.
With the generous protection of Great Britain they succeeded. Their
metropolis sent them settlers, technicians, educators, capital invest-
ments, and military support. A second Kingdom of Canada was born
and it was British.

The new inhabitants of Canada, who first called themselves the
British Americans, had hoped that they would completely assimilate
the *Canadiens*. After the 1820's, some shrewd leaders of British Canada
realized that it was impossible to achieve this aim. But they knew
that the *Canadiens* had no chance of remaining a majority in the
St. Lawrence valley. In fact, they were finally outnumbered by the
British during the fourth decade of the nineteenth century. There was
then no racial reason for delaying the granting of responsible government to the colony. The French-Canadian voters no longer threatened
British-Canadian domination. The British political leaders and businessmen had the assurance that they would forever run the country
they had built. The *Canadiens* had become a minority group whose
survival the British majority had come to tolerate, with more or less
good grace. Actually, they had no choice.

These are the bare facts. Now let us see what the social scientists
have said. William Smith, who wrote his *History of Canada* at the
beginning of the nineteenth century, gives an appalling description
of all the wrongs the *Canadiens* were supposed to have suffered during
the French régime and summons them to kneel before their British
benefactors who had conquered them only to liberate them: "How
happy, then, ought the Canadians to be, that God in his Providence,
has severed them from the ancient stock to which they belonged, and
committed them to the care of a Monarch, who, by making the success
of his arms the means of extending his beneficence, has an incon-
testible right to their affectionate fidelity."[1] In 1828, John Fleming, a
Montreal businessman and amateur historian, seriously maintained
that Great Britain had waged war against the *Canadiens* and taken
possession of their country "less from views of ambition and the
security of the other Colonies, than from the hope of improving their
situation, and endowing them with the privileges of freemen."[2]
Fleming's testimony was approvingly invoked by R. Montgomery
Martin in his history, *The British Colonies*, first published in the
1830's.[3]

Francis Parkman, one of the greatest romantic historians, did not

[1]William Smith, *History of Canada* (Québec, 1815), I, 383.
[2][John Fleming], *Political Annals of Lower Canada* (Montréal, 1828), lxxiii.
[3]R. Montgomery Martin, *The British Colonies* (London, n.d.), I, 15.

think differently. He believed that France could not give to the *Canadiens* the benefits of self-government because only the "German race, and especially the Anglo-Saxon branch of it, is particularly masculine, and, therefore, peculiarly fitted for self-government." As members of the French Empire, the "people of New France remained in a state of political segregation" and were kept in order by the armed forces of the king of France, according to Parkman. But, at last, the English Conquest

was the beginning of a new life. With England came Protestantism, and the Canadian church grew purer and better in the presence of an adverse faith. Material growth, an increased mental activity, an education real though fenced and guarded, a warm and genuine patriotism, all date from the peace of 1763. England imposed by the sword on reluctant Canada the boon of rational and ordered liberty. Through centuries of striving she had advanced from stage to stage of progress, deliberate and calm, never breaking with the past, but making each fresh gain the base of a new success, enlarging popular liberties while bating nothing of that height and force of individual development which is the brain and heart of civilization; and now, through a hard-earned victory, she taught the conquered colony to share the blessings she had won. A happier calamity never befell a people than the conquest of Canada by the British arms.[4]

Parkman sang this hymn to British liberty in 1874. Ten years later, he repeated that "civil liberty was given them [the *Canadiens*] by the British sword." However, his opinion of the Catholic Church had changed. He then regretted that the British conquerors had left the *Canadiens* free to exercise a religion that had transformed them into one of the "most priest-ridden communities of the modern world."[5] As a social scientist, Parkman should have known that the ecclesiastical pre-eminence he noted in French Canada, at the end of the nineteenth century, was one of the consequences of the British conquest and occupation. But how many social scientists have realized that?

William Kingsford, who published a ten volume *History of Canada* between 1887 and 1898, had nothing new to say. He had learned well the lesson taught by all his predecessors. According to his preconceptions and the accepted historical interpretation of his time, the *Canadiens* had been exploited and mistreated when Canada was a French colony. But the situation had rapidly changed under the "British rule which first awoke the French Canadian rural population to the duties, the obligations and independence of manhood."[6] Did

[4]Francis Parkman, *The Old Regime in Canada* (Boston, 1889), 397–8, 398, 395, 400–1. This book was first published in 1874. One must note that Parkman uses the challenge and response hypothesis. The latter has always been popular because it pleases the imagination, but scientifically speaking its value is very limited.
[5]Francis Parkman, *Montcalm and Wolfe: France and England in North America* (Centenary Edition, Boston, 1922), II, 427. This book was first published in 1884.
[6]William Kingsford, *The History of Canada*, IV (Toronto, 1890), 451.

Kingsford believe that the *Canadiens* had all been infants when they had lived alone in the St. Lawrence valley and fully enjoyed their freedom as a collectivity? In 1894, giving a survey of the colony around 1784, the same historian declared that the "rural population had remained unchanged in their social and political views, and shewed no inclination to accept the impulse of any modern movement."[7] Should we conclude that the awakening of the *Canadiens* to "the duties, the obligations and independence of manhood" under the benevolent guidance of their fatherly conquerors had not been completed after twenty-four years of British occupation? Were they so ungrateful and unintelligent that they refused to co-operate in their own liberation? Kingsford did not concern himself with these questions. With the over-confidence and naïveté of a Victorian imperialist convinced that the British Empire, in taking its share of the white man's burden, had a mission to civilize the backward *Canadiens*, he stated: "It is plain that whatever be the ethnological character of the French Canadians, that it has been under the British government that they have attained to the force and power they possess, and have moulded themselves to the type they present. The political liberty they have enjoyed has enabled them thus to increase in number and prosperity." To back up his assertions, he recalled that from 1632 to 1760 the *Canadiens* had increased to a total population of only 60,000 while from 1760 to 1888 (a period of 128 years like the preceding one), they had become a people of 1,250,000.[8] A high birth rate does not necessarily prove that a people is prosperous and free. Nor did the author take into account that the *Canadiens* had lived, since the Conquest, under the political and economic domination of the British *bourgeoisie*. Even if they were 1,250,000 strong in 1888, they were a minority group whose influence and resources were very limited when compared to those of the English population of Canada. A social scientist, who has an obligation to describe the actual situation of the collectivity he studies, is bound not to overlook, or hide, these fundamental facts.

Are the twentieth century historians and sociologists more realistic? Have they been able to renounce the political and social preconceptions of the romantic and Victorian eras? Old creeds endure, even among people who are responsible for the advancement of human knowledge. Man is so lazy that he does not easily change his mind. He feels so secure when he repeats the commonplaces and slogans of past generations. Smith, Fleming, Parkman, and Kingsford still continue to influence all the social scientists who write about French Canada, even those who have never read these old authors. The ideas of these earlier writers are part of an oral tradition which is carried

[7]*Ibid.*, VII, (1894), 195.   [8]*Ibid.*, IV, 502–3.

uncritically from one generation to the next. Nor does such a process only occur, as we are inclined to believe, among the lower and more ignorant classes. It happens frequently, too frequently indeed, in academic circles, where young scholars let themselves be directed into the well-worn tracks of their teachers.

Among the modern historians Professor A. L. Burt has devoted many years of his scholarly life to the study of Canada after the British Conquest. His book, *The Old Province of Quebec*, is still one of the major works in Canadian history. The author has enlarged our knowledge of this period. Unfortunately, he has contributed nothing new on the French-Canadian problem. Like all his predecessors, he has failed to see what was the actual position of the *Canadiens*, as a collectivity, before and after the British Conquest. He goes so far as to maintain that they "had been forced to live an unnatural life under governors of their own blood, but under rulers of an alien race they were to find themselves."[9] He is sincerely convinced that the British occupation benefited the "French in Canada [who] were the first considerable body of an alien race to taste that liberty which is larger than English liberty and is the secret of the modern British commonwealth of nations."[10] For him, the *Canadiens* obtained from their conquerors the "liberty to be themselves."[11] How can a people living under the domination of a conqueror be free? Has not Professor Burt himself noted that the *Canadiens* on the eve of the War of 1812, after more than sixty years of British liberty, "were now openly resenting the rule of their British masters."[12] One can then suppose that they did not feel that they had the "liberty to be themselves." In fact, they began to resent the British rule immediately after the Conquest.[13] Their reaction was that of any collectivity living under the yoke of its former enemies. It cannot be otherwise. How can a social scientist overlook this fact?

Professor Edgar McInnis, whose textbook on Canadian history is perhaps the best yet published, realizes that the British businessmen, enjoying a privileged situation, "stepped right into the key positions in the economic life of the province of Quebec, and that fact made them of salient importance in political affairs as well."[14] If the words he uses have any meaning, one must infer that the *Canadiens* were com-

---

[9]A. L. Burt, *The Old Province of Quebec* (Toronto, 1933), 12.   [10]*Ibid.*, 56.

[11]The title of the fifth chapter of A. L. Burt's textbook, *A Short History of Canada for Americans* (Minneapolis, 1942 and 1944), 57.

[12]A. L. Burt, *The United States, Great Britain and British North America from the Revolution to the Establishment of the Peace after the War of 1812* (Toronto, 1940), 319.

[13]See Michel Brunet, "Les Canadiens après la Conquête: Les débuts de la résistance passive," *Revue d'histoire de l'Amérique française*, XII (sept. 1958), 170–207.

[14]Edgar McInnis, *Canada: A Political and Social History* (Toronto, 1947), 131.

pelled to bow down before the economic and political domination of the British invaders. This is actually what happened. But the author does not seem to take into account what he himself has written for he asserts a few lines below: "The French had much cause to feel that their fortunes had been improved by the change of masters."[15] Like all his predecessors, Professor McInnis does not realize that the *Canadiens*, when they lived alone in the St. Lawrence valley, were their own masters. Their relationship with France was that of a colonial nation with her metropolis which worked, in collaboration with the colonial leaders, for their collective benefit. Associated by force with the British Empire, they were reduced to the status of a subjected people. Great Britain had not conquered Canada for the good of the *Canadiens* but for the development of British colonization in North America.

Every book published by Professor D. G. Creighton is a landmark in Canadian historiography. In reaction to the nationalist school of historians who had over-emphasized the English Canadians' struggle to achieve self-government and depicted Great Britain as the villain of the story, he has shown what is the actual basis of Canadian separateness in North America and how great is English Canada's debt to its mother country. On many topics of Canadian history, his authority is, and shall remain, unchallenged. However, his approach to French Canada is still that of Parkman's. He declares: "To the defeated society of the north it [the British Conquest] brought fresh enthusiasm, a new strength and a different leadership. But this injection of new vigour, while it strengthened commercial Canada, necessarily raised the problem of assimilation."[16] How can a "defeated society," placed under the domination of an alien *bourgeoisie* and engaged in a process of assimilation by its conquerors, become stronger? For Professor Creighton, the *Canadiens'* opposition to their conquerors' rule was merely a "struggle between commercialism represented aggressively by the merchants and a decadent semi-feudal society defended by peasants and professional men."[17] The *Canadiens*, for various reasons, having not been completely assimilated by the British inhabitants of the St. Lawrence valley, Professor Creighton asks himself if the Conquest has not given a "chance that an older, simpler, more devout France, the France of the seventeenth, not of the eighteenth, century, would maintain its footing and even increase its influence in North America?"[18] A society is a living organism, not a

[15]*Ibid.*, 132.

[16]Donald G. Creighton, *The Empire of the St. Lawrence* (Toronto, 1956), 21. This book was first published in 1937.   [17]*Ibid.*, 126.

[18]Donald G. Creighton, *Dominion of the North: A History of Canada* (Boston, 1944), 144.

museum. Is it possible to compare the influence which the *Canadiens* have had since 1760, in the St. Lawrence valley and in North America, to that they exerted at the time of the French North American Empire?

Among contemporary Canadian historians, Professor A. R. M. Lower has made a commendable effort to understand French-Canadian collective behaviour. But his interpretation of French Canada's history follows the traditional path. He has come to the startling conclusion that: "What saved French liberty was its loss—its loss in the English conquest, for out of conquest came eventually the English institutional apparatus of freedom—popular government and all the guarantees of the common law. . . . If the rule of France had not been terminated, New France in the course of time might or might not have drifted off to some kind of independence: what it would not have done would have been to secure the institutions of freedom with which it is now familiar."[19] Does Professor Lower prefer the "English institutional apparatus of freedom" to freedom itself? As a political scientist who has studied with enthusiasm the liberal democratic way of life, he knows that a people cannot leave to another people the care of its liberty because, as he himself explains, "liberty left to others to look after turns out to be slavery."[20] A conquered nation that is unable to drive out the invaders and finally becomes a minority group in its native land loses its right to self-determination. For it, there is no independence. Professor Lower should have realized this when he once wrote: "Conquest is a type of slavery. . . . The entire life-structure of the conquered is laid open to their masters. They become second-rate people."[21] It is evident that this author has not meditated long enough upon the historical facts submitted to his observation or the political principles he has himself enunciated. No other Anglo-Canadian historian was in a better position to describe accurately the fate of the *Canadiens*.

Sociologists who have studied the French-Canadian collectivity have simply repeated the historians.[22] One must not criticize them too severely because, after all, what can sociologists do when historians

[19]Arthur R. M. Lower, *Canada: Nation and Neighbour* (Toronto, 1952), 49.
[20]A. R. M. Lower, *This Most Famous Stream: The Liberal Democratic Way of Life* (Toronto, 1954), 9.
[21]A. R. M. Lower, *Colony to Nation: A History of Canada* (Toronto, 1946), 63.
[22]See Everett C. Hughes, *Rencontre de deux mondes: La crise d'industrialisation du Canada français* (Montréal, 1944), 13. (This book was published in 1943 under the English title, *French Canada in Transition*, and translated into French by Professor Jean-Charles Falardeau, Director of the Department of Sociology at Laval University); Everett C. and Helen M. Hughes, *Where Peoples Meet: Racial and Ethnic Frontiers* (Glencoe, Ill., 1952), 114; Horace Miner, *St. Denis, a French-Canadian Parish* (Chicago, 1939).

give them false references about the past history of the society they observe?[23] Without the background knowledge that historians alone can furnish, sociologists are powerless. Professor Everett C. Hughes and all his disciples (and they are numerous) have much difficulty in trying to prove that the *Canadiens* have formed a folk society since the seventeenth century. In accordance with the old historical interpretation, these writers have convinced themselves that the British Conquest and occupation did not modify the social structure of French Canada. On the other hand, they realize that French Canadians, as a group, are in a position of subordination. They have discovered the explanation for this situation. For them, the *Canadiens* are struggling under the impact of twentieth-century industrialization. The former folk society of French Canada is crumbling and its members are painfully adapting themselves to the industrial and urban age. So speak the sociologists and anthropologists. They all agree that it is a toilsome and slow social process. A few among them think that French-Canadian society will melt away by integration and acculturation. These new pedantic and mysterious words are now used to name a social phenomenon which was formerly called, more accurately, assimilation. Others are more optimistic and seem sure that the *Canadiens* will overcome this ordeal. The political, economic, social, and cultural problems to which industrialization and urbanization give rise present a challenge to any society. There is no exception for French Canada. But one must never lose sight of the fact that a foreign conquest and occupation is the greatest impact a society can ever meet. How can social scientists ignore this fact when they study French Canada? Moreover, the Redfield school of sociologists should know that the *Canadiens* have never formed a folk society!

French Canadians themselves have been unable, for two centuries, to understand the actual causes of their ordeal as a collectivity. The first spokesmen of French Canada, after the Conquest, were obliged to collaborate with the British authorities under whose thumb they now had to live. They developed the habit of flattering their conquerors with the hope of gaining their protection. They gradually adopted all the commonplaces, watchwords, and slogans of their British masters about the rights of Englishmen and the exceptional merits of the British constitution. They spoke with scorn of the French régime

[23]See also the statements of the following historians: Frank Basil Tracy, *The Tercentenary History of Canada* (Toronto, 1908), II, 557, 562; Mary Quayle Innis, *An Economic History of Canada* (Toronto, 1935), 63; John Bartlet Brebner, *The North Atlantic Triangle* (Toronto, 1945), 32–5, 48–9; G. P. de T. Glazebrook, *A Short History of Canada* (Oxford, 1950), 82, 90; Gerald S. Graham, *Canada: A Short History* (London, 1950), 63, 74; J. M. S. Careless, *Canada: A Story of Challenge* (Cambridge, 1953), 93, 100; Mason Wade, *The French Canadians, 1760–1945* (Toronto, 1955), 44, 47–8, 88.

knowing very well that such a language pleased the government and the British merchants. Indeed, the *Canadiens* who were responsible for dealing with the British administration and *bourgeoisie* were not free to act or think differently. They had to conciliate the invaders who occupied their country. The result was that after one generation, the leaders of French Canada had almost assimilated all the official thinking of their British rulers.

The Church did much to contribute to the dissemination of this British propaganda. One must always remember that the ecclesiastical administrators, whose influence was now very great in a society deprived of its natural lay leaders, became the most faithful supporters of the British domination immediately after the Conquest. By granting the Church a few privileges, the conquerors skilfully secured their devotion. The French Revolution strengthened this bond. The priesthood and all church-going *Canadiens* came to the conclusion that God himself had favoured the British Conquest of Canada in order to protect the Catholic Church of this country and the *nation canadienne* from the abuses and horrors of this wicked revolution. The British did their best to propagate this providential interpretation of their coming to the St. Lawrence valley. The French royalist priests whom the London government encouraged to immigrate to Canada from 1792 to 1802 were very useful to this end. Many generations of *Canadiens* have asked themselves with alarm what would have been their fate if they had been members of the French Empire during the revolutionary era. Even today, this question still troubles some conservative minded French-Canadian leaders who have not yet rejected the legends their forefathers believed in.

A speech delivered by Louis-Joseph Papineau, then Speaker of the House of Lower Canada, on the occasion of the death of George III, reveals to what extent the leaders of the conquered *Canadiens* had embraced the political thinking of their masters:

George III, a sovereign respected for his moral qualities and his devotion to his duties, succeeded Louis XV, a prince justly despised for his debauches, for his lack of attention to the needs of the people, and for his senseless prodigality to his favorites and mistresses. Since that epoch the reign of law has succeeded to that of violence; since that day the treasure, the fleet, and the armies of Great Britain have been employed to provide us with an effective protection against all foreign danger; since that day her best laws have become ours, while our faith, our property, and the laws by which they were governed have been conserved; soon afterwards the privileges of her free constitution were granted us, infallible guarantees of our domestic prosperity if it is observed. Now religious tolerance; trial by jury, the wisest guarantee which has ever been established for the protection of innocence; security against arbitrary imprisonment, thanks to the privilege of the *habeas corpus*; equal protection guaranteed by law to the person, honor, and property of citizens; the right to obey only laws made by us and adopted by our representatives—all these advantages have become our birthright, and will be, I hope, the lasting heritage of our posterity. In order to conserve them, we should act like British subjects and free men.[24]

Papineau made no distinction between individual rights and collective freedom. Under the British domination, the *Canadiens* enjoyed the right of property, although in this respect, one must not forget the confiscation of the Jesuits' estates and all the wrongs the other religous communities suffered; they could exercise their religion, but the bishop and all ecclesiastical administrators were subjected to close and suspicious supervision by the colonial and imperial authorities.[25] They were entitled to a fair trial when arrested, and they elected representatives to a House of Assembly with very limited powers. Indeed, there is no reason to cry out in admiration of the British administration. But the "English institutional apparatus of freedom" did impress Papineau for a while. When he tried to give some meaning to British liberty and claimed for the *Canadiens*, who constituted the majority of the population in Lower Canada, the right to govern themselves, he and his followers were crushed by British military forces. If the *Canadiens* had been entrusted with the government of the St. Lawrence valley, it would have seriously jeopardized the future of British colonization in North America. Lower and Upper Canada were united. The *Canadiens*, now reduced to the status of a minority group, had to accept the leadership of the British Americans who took control of the government of a united Canada. Papineau, LaFontaine, Morin, and all the other French-Canadian leaders of the 1840's did not understand what had actually happened. Some of them were naïve enough to believe that they had obtained for their people the right to self-government. The French-Canadian leaders who have since succeeded them have laboured under the same delusion. They boast that they have achieved Canada's independence for the *Canadiens!*
Social scientists of French Canada have not been more clear-sighted than its politicians. Men of action are not bound to analyse the social and political evolution of the collectivity. They have other problems to face and to solve. However, historians, political scientists, and sociologists have the task of giving a true picture of the society they study. With the exception of François Xavier-Garneau who partly realized what had been the consequences of the British Conquest for the *Canadiens* as a people,[26] French-Canadian historians have, in

[24]The speech was delivered in July 1820; quoted in Wade, *French Canadians*, 127–8.
[25]For example, the bishop was forbidden to convene a synod, and he could not travel abroad.
[26]See François-Xavier Garneau, *Histoire du Canada* (4 vols., Québec, 1845–52), III, 296, 303–4; IV, 313.

general, adopted with only a few slight differences the historical interpretation of the American and English-Canadian scholars.[27] This fact is a striking one and it has never been adequately pointed out. It indicates that the French-Canadian upper classes have been engaged, since the Conquest, in a process of assimilation to English Canada. The assimilation of one people by another always begins with its leaders. But one has also to take into consideration that the teaching of social sciences has long been and is still neglected in French-Canadian universities. Laval University, founded in 1852, and the University of Montreal, a mere branch of Laval from 1876 to 1920, have never had the intellectual traditions and the financial resources required to become genuine institutions of higher learning. The situation has somewhat improved during the last ten years but there are still too few French-Canadian scholars carrying on fresh investigations in the social sciences. The low standard of education in French Canada has been one of the numerous misfortunes which befell the *Canadiens* since the Conquest of their homeland.[28] Too many people —not always ill-intentioned—who have deplored or denounced the ignorance of the *Canadiens* have overlooked the fact that, from 1760 to the second half of the nineteenth century, they were unable to organize a decent school system. France could no longer send them the teachers they needed and the French government had discontinued its financial grants to education. On the other hand, the *Canadiens* could not count on the help of the British authorities. Is it necessary to recall the fate of the College of Quebec?

Social scientists from both French and English Canada, and foreign students of French-Canadian history, have all failed to describe the actual situation of the *Canadiens* as a people because their frame of reference was inadequate. They have never seriously asked themselves how a society forms itself—especially a colonial society—and under what conditions it comes to maturity. How can it be arrested in its

27See Michel Bibaud, *Histoire du Canada sous la domination française* (Montréal, 1843), 414; and *Histoire du Canada et des Canadiens sous la domination anglaise* (Montréal, 1844), 5; G.-H. Macaulay, *Passé, présent et avenir du Canada* (Montréal, 1859), 6; Philippe Aubert de Gaspé, *Les Anciens Canadiens* (Québec, 1863), 202; *Les Ursulines de Québec depuis leur établissement jusqu'à nos jours* (Québec, 1863–6), III, 349; J.-S. Raymond, "Enseignements des événements contemporains," *Revue canadienne*, VIII (1871), 55; Benjamin Sulte, *Histoire des Canadiens-Français* (Montréal, 1882–4), VII, 134; L.-F.-G. Baby, "L'exode des classes dirigeantes à la cession du Canada," *The Canadian Antiquarian and Numismatic Journal*, 3rd series, II (1899), 127; Desrosiers et Fournet, *La Race française en Amérique* (Montréal, 1910), 292; Thomas Chapais, *Cours d'histoire du Canada* (Québec, 1919–40), I, 3–5; Lionel Groulx, *Lendemains de conquête* (Montréal, 1920), 182, 183, 216, 232–3, 235; Gustave Lanctôt, "Situation politique de l'Eglise canadienne sous le régime français," *Rapports de la Société canadienne d'histoire de l'Eglise catholique*, VIII (1940–1), 56.
28See Lionel Groulx, *L'Enseignement français au Canada* (Montréal, 1933), I, 37–58.

development and reduced to a status of mere survival? Why does a society disappear? These are the essential questions a social scientist must bring forward and answer to fulfil his responsibility as a scholar. Unfortunately, the social sciences have not yet shaken off the limitations of amateurism and romanticism. Social scientists are too often literary men who become students of society by accident, and their approach is often that of the novelist.

Factors of an emotional nature have also exerted a very bad influence on the thinking of French- and English-Canadian historians. The latter were in a very ticklish position. Could they admit that the British Conquest and occupation of the St. Lawrence valley had wronged the *Canadiens* as a people? Being rightly proud of the British businessmen and settlers who have built, with the help of Great Britain, the second Kingdom of Canada, their first objective was to relate their achievements with a patriotic bent. The history of French Canada did not interest them very much and they did not care to study is seriously. But they could not completely ignore the fact of the Conquest. Having a feeling of solidarity with the conquerors, they were inclined to vindicate their actions. Finally, they easily convinced themselves that the fate of the *Canadiens* had been better under the British rule than it would have been if they had remained in the French Empire. This hypothesis was a mere subterfuge but it had the advantage of giving good conscience to the English-Canadian majority. All conquerors use arguments of this kind to legitimize their domination over a subjected people. One must never forget that France had not conquered French Canada but had founded it and that the *Canadiens* could not develop normally as a people without the help of their metropolis. However, English-Canadian social scientists can be excused. Were not the principal spokesmen of French Canada—the bishops, political leaders, businessmen, and historians—all eager to proclaim that, after all, the coming of the British had benefited Canada and the *Canadiens*?

Indeed, the churchmen and lawyer-politicians who, for six generations, have led the French Canadians, like to believe that the Conquest did not impair the growth of their compatriots as a people. They stubbornly refuse to recognize that the *Canadiens* are conquered people whose survival as a collectivity has been possible because the conquerors were unable to assimilate them completely. On the contrary, they have endeavoured to persuade themselves that the challenge of the British occupation has even contributed to the strength of French Canada. It is said that the *Canadiens* have learned how to avail themselves of the prosperity and liberty the British are supposed to have brought to Canada. All agree that there were some difficulties in the beginning, and that a few wicked British wanted to persecute the *Canadiens* and to assimilate them. But the *Canadiens* are told that, thanks to the cleverness of their religious and political leaders and their own courage, they have finally successfully overcome all the bad consequences of a foreign domination. The French-Canadian ruling classes, whose accession to their position of pre-eminence has always been dependent on the willingness of either the British authorities or the English-Canadian leaders, are interested in upholding this historical interpretation. Nor does this viewpoint displease too much the English-Canadian majority whose good conscience is not upset. It gives to the priesthood and politicians of French Canada the rôle of Saviours in the service of their people. It also magnifies the *Canadiens'* national pride. In any society vested interests and patriotic emotions tend to influence the writings and teaching of the social scientists. Too often they themselves are unaware of this social pressure.

The era of amateurism and romanticism is over. It is time to put Parkman aside. Social scientists should leave to the politicians and preachers the job of making pep-talks about the grandeur and virtues of British liberty, free enterprise, rugged individualism, and similar topics. They must approach the study of society with more scientific methods. They must state with candour and lucidity all the problems and challenges of our times.

In Canada, French- and English-Canadian social scientists bear heavy responsibilities. They must be conversant with all the political, economic, and social problems facing the Atlantic world in the second half of the twentieth century. Men of action who are entrusted with the orientation of Canada need their help to perform their duty. And there is in this country a peculiar problem that challenges every generation of Canadian citizens: the peaceful coexistence of the *Canadiens* and Canadians. This coexistence has begun almost two centuries ago. It seems that it will endure for many more generations.

Can we say that social scientists have up to now been equal to their task in dealing with this sociological problem? Was not their approach to it quite unsatisfactory? Their wishful thinking and their romanticism have impeded their examination of the fundamental facts that have determined the historical and sociological evolution of Canada. They have never perceived the true nature of the relations which have existed, since the Conquest, between *Canadiens* and Canadians. They do not even have the excuse of having promoted "national unity." A true and fruitful partnership between French and English Canadians cannot be based upon a common misunderstanding of Canadian history and Canadian society. Empty words about democracy, self-government, *bonne entente,* and the riches which a bilingual and bicultural state is supposed to enjoy have too often deceived the social scientists of Canada. They have first the obligation to analyse the facts without troubling themselves with the vested interests they will hurt or the unfavourable reactions of the influential people they will scandalize. For the good of Canada, and Atlantic civilization itself, they have the opportunity, by studying with a fresh approach our own historical and social problems, to make a worthy contribution to the progress of the social sciences.